COMPACT *Research*

Gun Control

by George A. Milite

Current Issues

ReferencePoint
Press™

San Diego, CA

For more information, contact
ReferencePoint Press, Inc.
PO Box 27779
San Diego, CA 92198
www.ReferencePointPress.com

Picture Credits:
AP/Wide World Photos, 9 (inset), 11
Getty Images, 9
Maury Aaseng, 32–35, 47–49, 62–65, 75–77

Series design:
Tamia Dowlatabadi

LIBRARY OF CONGRESS CATALOGING-IN-PUBLICATION DATA

Milite, George A.
  Gun control / by George A. Milite.
    p. cm. — (Compact research series)
  Includes bibliographical references and index.
  ISBN-13: 978-1-60152-010-4 (hardback)
  ISBN-10: 1-60152-010-7 (hardback)
  1. Gun control—United States. 2. Firearms ownership—United States. 3. Violence—United States. I. Title.
  HV7436.M54 2006
  363.330973--dc22

                                                                              2006032873

Contents

Foreword

> 66 **Where is the knowledge we have lost in information?** 99
>
> —"The Rock," T.S. Eliot

As modern civilization continues to evolve, its ability to create, store, distribute, and access information expands exponentially. The explosion of information from all media continues to increase at a phenomenal rate. By 2020 some experts predict the worldwide information base will double every 73 days. While access to diverse sources of information and perspectives is paramount to any democratic society, information alone cannot help people gain knowledge and understanding. Information must be organized and presented clearly and succinctly in order to be understood. The challenge in the digital age becomes not the creation of information, but how best to sort, organize, enhance, and present information.

ReferencePoint Press developed the Compact Research series with this challenge of the information age in mind. More than any other subject area today, researching current events can yield vast, diverse, and unqualified information that can be intimidating and overwhelming for even the most advanced and motivated researcher. The Compact Research series offers a compact, relevant, intelligent, and conveniently organized collection of information covering a variety of current and controversial topics ranging from illegal immigration to marijuana.

The series focuses on three types of information: objective single-author narratives, opinion-based primary source quotations, and facts and statistics. The clearly written objective narratives provide context and reliable background information. Primary source quotes are carefully selected and cited, exposing the reader to differing points of view. And facts and statistics sections aid the reader in evaluating perspectives. Presenting these key types of information creates a richer, more balanced learning experience.

For better understanding and convenience, the series enhances information by organizing it into narrower topics and adding design features that make it easy for a reader to identify desired content. For example, in *Compact Research: Illegal Immigration*, a chapter covering the economic impact of illegal immigration has an objective narrative explaining the various ways the economy is impacted, a balanced section of numerous primary source quotes on the topic, followed by facts and full-color illustrations to encourage evaluation of contrasting perspectives.

The ancient Roman philosopher Lucius Annaeus Seneca wrote, "It is quality rather than quantity that matters." More than just a collection of content, the Compact Research series is simply committed to creating, finding, organizing, and presenting the most relevant and appropriate amount of information on a current topic in a user-friendly style that invites, intrigues, and fosters understanding.

Gun Control at a Glance

Prevalence of Guns

Nearly 39 percent of all households in the United States have a gun.

Crime

Sixty-five percent of all homicides in 2003 were committed with guns, suggesting a link between the millions of guns in private hands and gun-related crime.

Guns and Teens

Although many states have laws prohibiting the sale of guns to minors, the largest number of gun crimes in the United States are committed by 18- to 20-year-olds.

Illegal Guns

An estimated 1.7 million guns were stolen between 1993 and 2002. Many of these end up in the black market and are used to commit crimes.

Guns and the Second Amendment

The Second Amendment to the Constitution guarantees the right to bear arms but is vague about whether that right extends to private citizens.

Gun Laws

There are some 22,000 federal, state, and municipal gun laws in the United States. The high rate of gun crime nationally suggests that many gun laws have little effect.

Background Checks

Between 1998 and 2005 the FBI conducted nearly 60 million background checks on potential gun buyers and denied purchases to 450,000.

Overview: Understanding the Debate

On September 27, 2006, Duane Morison, a petty criminal, walked into a school in Bailey, Colorado, armed with 2 guns. He took six students hostage and killed 1 before killing himself. Two days later, Eric Hainstock, a 15-year-old high school student, walked into his Cazenovia, Wisconsin, school armed with two guns. Quick-thinking school staff stopped the boy, but the effort cost the life of 1 teacher. Three days after that, in the Amish community of Nickel Mines, Pennsylvania, a milk-truck driver named Charles Carl Roberts walked into a 1-room schoolhouse carrying a pistol, a rifle, and a 12-gauge shotgun. He tied up 10 schoolgirls and shot them all; 5 died almost instantly.

These three tragic events could serve as arguments either for or against gun control. Advocates of gun control believe that if guns were more difficult to obtain or less plentiful, these three gunmen (and others like them) might never have gotten hold of guns. Those who support the right of individuals to own firearms, however, believe that law-abiding citizens who own guns and who use them responsibly are the ones who would suffer from stricter gun control laws. The behavior of those who commit gun violence is no reason to punish responsible gun owners.

Gun control is a polarizing issue, one that spurs a raw emotional response. Deborah Homsher, author of *Women and Guns: Politics and the Culture of Firearms in America*, notes that "public discussion about gun control has been conducted as a war, with insults, exaggerations, and caricatures deployed by both sides, often as a means to ignite passionate fundraising campaigns."[1] Both proponents and opponents of gun control are aware of the tragic consequences that can arise from gun violence.

In 2006, in an Amish community in Pennsylvania, a milk-truck driver named Charles Carl Roberts walked into a one-room schoolhouse, tied up 10 schoolgirls and shot them before killing himself. This incident reignited the debate over increased gun control to help prevent such horrible crimes.

The difference—and it is a difference worth understanding and respecting—is that there are people who believe sincerely that gun laws either do or do not prevent such tragedies.

The literature on both sides is filled with poignant stories about death and injury. The victim could be a child, a grandfather, a young college woman, or a loving husband celebrating his wedding anniversary with his wife. Suddenly the victim is confronted by a person or persons brandishing guns—perhaps a robber, maybe a carjacker. Shots are fired and innocent people are killed or wounded. The survivors' lives are never the same.

Gun control proponents always end such stories with an admonition that if the shooters had only been prevented from having a gun, the tragedy would never have happened. Those who oppose gun control, however, always end such stories with the sober observation that if those innocent victims had themselves been armed, they could have defended themselves against harm. Although the stories add a vividness to the issue that facts and figures cannot, the truth is that both sides make valid points about gun ownership.

> There is general agreement that the average individual does not need a high-powered weapon for everyday use.

What Is Gun Control?

Gun control is a broad term that refers to a variety of methods for curtailing the availability of guns. It can include prohibiting all private citizens from owning firearms, placing restrictions on certain types of weapons, or restricting who can own or purchase those weapons. The bottom line on gun control is that it is meant to reduce the danger that firearms—handguns, shotguns, rifles, and assault weapons—can inflict on the public.

There are a number of gun control strategies that have been used at the federal, state, and local levels over the years. One is imposing restrictions on the types of guns purchased. Certain guns, including automatic and semiautomatic weapons (which can rapidly fire numerous rounds of ammunition), have long been restricted for purchase or possession. There is general agreement that the average individual does not need a high-powered weapon for everyday use.

Another approach is imposing restrictions on the number of guns one can purchase. A number of states and municipalities have enacted "one gun a month" laws that restrict the number of guns an individual can purchase over a specific period of time. In California, Maryland, and Virginia, for example, an individual can purchase only one gun every 30 days. This prevents people from stockpiling weapons, and it also prevents potential gunrunners from purchasing a large number of guns to sell illegally.

Restricting the purchase of ammunition is yet another tactic. Some laws have been developed to limit the amount of ammunition individuals can buy. In Chicago, for example, so-called assault ammunition (any ammunition magazine that can fire more than 12 rounds) is banned for transfer, acquisition, or possession. Also, laws have been passed banning the sale or possession of "armor-piercing" bullets that can go through bulletproof vests (which are frequently used by police).

Licensing restrictions have been imposed by various states for years. Some states and municipalities require gun purchasers to fill out detailed

In 2004 Chicago mayor Richard Daley walks past a table of confiscated automatic assault weapons after urging the U.S. government to renew a 10-year ban on semiautomatic assault weapons. The ban was not renewed and expired September 13, 2004.

forms before they can purchase a gun; often, these forms must be accompanied by a fee. New York City has one of the strictest gun registration requirements in the country. Anyone who wishes to purchase a gun must not only fill out detailed forms that state exactly how the firearm will be used but also pay fees totaling more than $400. The most restrictive license, the "Premises License," allows the license holder to have a handgun only at his or her residence or place of business; the gun cannot leave the premises except under lock and key (handgun and ammunition in separate, locked containers). Also, some licenses allow specific firearms to be used only in specific places or situations. Having these forms makes it easier for government agencies to keep records and conduct background checks.

Waiting Periods

The amount of time between a gun purchase and the purchaser's actual possession of a gun allows authorities to do criminal background checks and determine whether the purchaser is legally eligible to carry or own a gun. Some states and municipalities require waiting periods of several weeks; New York requires a waiting period of up to six months to obtain a license. In other states, such as Wyoming, however, there are no waiting periods of any kind on the books.

> The amount of time between a gun purchase and the purchaser's actual possession of a gun allows authorities to do criminal background checks.

The federal government has enacted gun control strategies over the years, the best known of which is the Brady Handgun Violence Prevention Act of 1993, known more commonly as the Brady Bill. As initially structured, the law (which went into effect in 1994) required a five-day waiting period for anyone who wished to purchase a handgun in the United States. This five-day waiting period allowed a gun dealer to make sure the purchaser's identification information was accurate. During those five days, dealers could find out if the potential purchaser had a criminal record, for instance; this would prevent guns from falling into the hands of felons (who are banned by law from purchasing firearms).

The Brady Bill came about largely because of the work of Sarah and James Brady over a period of more than a decade. In March 1981 James Brady, then press secretary to President Ronald Reagan, was severely wounded by gunman John Hinckley during an assassination attempt on the president. Brady nearly died from his wounds and was permanently paralyzed on one side. He and his wife Sarah fought for what they believed would be more commonsense gun control regulations. The five-day waiting period came about because Hinckley, who had suffered from mental illness, put a phony address on his gun application when he bought the handgun that wounded Brady. Had he been subject to a waiting period, the Bradys contended, he might not have been sold a handgun.

> "Another approach [to gun control] is imposing restrictions on the number of guns one can purchase."

The 5-day waiting period was a temporary requirement while the Federal Bureau of Investigation (FBI) came up with a more comprehensive nationwide checking system. That program, the National Instant Criminal Background Check System (NICS), was launched in November 1998. All gun sellers (known as federal firearms licensees, or FFLs) are required to run background checks on individuals attempting to purchase a firearm. Today, more than half the states use NICS exclusively; the others access the NICS database through their own state agencies. The waiting period under NICS is shorter than under the initial Brady Bill (3 days instead of 5), but NICS checks include "long guns" (such as rifles) whereas the Brady Bill only covered handguns. Some states have longer waiting periods than NICS requires.

According to the FBI, as of the end of 2005 some 450,000 individuals who were ineligible to own guns had been prohibited from purchasing them thanks to NICS. Those individuals included people convicted of felony (and some misdemeanor) crimes, anyone subject to a restraining order, anyone who had been imprisoned for substance abuse, people who had been dishonorably discharged from the military, and illegal aliens.

Who Owns Guns?

The exact number of gun owners is difficult to determine, but estimates put the figure as high as 80 million—nearly one-third of the population of the United States. There are many different kinds of gun owners who have a variety of reasons for owning firearms.

Hunters are one of the most visible groups of gun owners in America. It is estimated that some 18 million individuals in the United States hunt. Hunters are among the most carefully regulated shooters in the United States. They are required to obtain permits that allow them to hunt specific animals in specific seasons and only in designated areas. This is done for a number of reasons: It protects animals (killing nursing animal mothers in the spring would mean that their offspring might starve);

> " The exact number of gun owners is difficult to determine but estimates put the figure as high as 80 million—nearly one third of the population of the United States. "

it protects innocent bystanders (a hunter cannot come into someone's yard to shoot at a deer); it also protects the hunters themselves (too many hunters in the same area could result in accidents). Hunters have a reputation for being extremely responsible with their weapons. They also have a reputation for being among the nation's most active conservationists, donating an estimated $1.5 billion annually to wildlife conservation organizations.

Target shooters are another group of gun owners. A popular sport for centuries, target shooting is even an Olympic event; shooting competitions have been featured at the Summer Olympic Games since 1896. There are an estimated 19 million Americans who shoot for sport; these shooters use handguns, shotguns, and rifles, and their goal is to increase their shooting speed and accuracy.

Collectors are another important group of gun owners. Although there are no actual figures for how large a group this is, there are hundreds of gun collectors' organizations in the United States. As with any item that requires a high degree of craftsmanship, guns and other firearms are popular with collectors. (Many collectors also collect ammunition.) The typical gun collector looks for items that come from a particular manufacturer or a specific time period (such as a war); the rarer the gun, the more valuable it is. Gun collectors may also own working guns, but they do not shoot their collectible firearms.

Many people buy guns for self-defense. They see guns as an ideal means of defense against burglary, robbery, or more serious crimes. Some people may have one handgun, while others may keep several weapons. Many people who purchase guns for self-defense count on the "surprise factor"; most would-be criminals, they feel, will flee merely at the sight of a gun rather than risk getting shot themselves.

Types of Guns

The most common (and probably best-known) guns are handguns, which include revolvers, pistols, and derringers. Even some semiautomatic and automatic guns can be considered handguns, as long as they can be held in one hand. (Semiautomatic weapons allow one cartridge at a time to be shot but will reload the next cartridge as soon as one is fired. Automatic weapons, such as machine guns and other assault weapons, are those that will shoot cartridges as long as the trigger is held.) There are an estimated 70 million handguns in the United States. The typical handgun is the most common firearm both because it is relatively easy to buy and easy to conceal.

Rifles and shotguns, known as "long guns" because of their long barrels, are popular for those who put a high value on accuracy. (The long barrel is more accurate at longer ranges.) Hunters and target shooters—who look for accuracy rather than easy concealment—use long guns.

> " Hunters are among the most carefully regulated shooters in the United States. "

Automatic weapons such as machine guns are used primarily by the military. Under the Firearm Owners Protection Act of 1986, civilians are prohibited from purchasing machine guns manufactured after 1986, and under the Gun Control Act of 1968 machine guns cannot be imported for civilian sale.

Guns and Crime

The role firearms play in criminal activity, and what to do about them, is one of the biggest sticking points between those who support gun control and those who support gun ownership. According to the FBI, in 2005 some 125,000 violent crimes (including murder, rape, robbery, and assault) were committed in the United States with firearms. Of the 10,100 murders committed with firearms, 7,543 were committed with handguns. Both proponents and opponents of gun control agree that this figure is too high and want to see it reduced. How to reduce the figure is what they disagree about.

Advocates for gun control claim that the huge number of guns in existence makes it easier for criminals to acquire them through theft. They believe that the way to reduce gun crime is to make guns less readily available. Whether through waiting periods, stricter licensing requirements, tighter background checks, or more restrictions on actual guns, the key is to reduce the number of available guns that criminals can get their hands on.

Those who advocate gun ownership say that the criminals are precisely the problem; if they were arrested and sentenced adequately, they would not be around to steal guns, the market for illegal guns would shrink, and there would be less gun violence.

Advocates believe that existing laws on the books are more than sufficient to handle gun crime. (There are an estimated 22,000 federal, state, and municipal gun laws in the United States.) They argue that enforcing those laws and going after criminals more diligently is what will reduce gun crime and that more controls on guns will merely punish law-abiding gun owners.

There are an estimated 70 million handguns in the United States.

President George W. Bush concurs with this line of reasoning. During the October 13, 2004, presidential debate with Senator John Kerry in Tempe, Arizona, Bush said, "The best way to protect our citizens from guns is to prosecute those who commit crimes with guns."[2]

Opponents of gun control say that more effective and uniform enforcement of existing laws will have the strongest impact on gun violence. Tracking down and arresting illegal gun dealers is one such step. So is cracking down on "straw purchases." (A straw purchase occurs when a person with no criminal background purchases a gun for someone whose background prohibits gun ownership.)

Is There Common Ground?

Both sides of the gun control debate have staunch supporters—gun control advocates who want guns to be regulated almost out of existence and gun owners who want no restrictions even against machine guns or other large-scale weapons. As John R. Lott Jr., a legal scholar who has done extensive research on the relationship between guns and crime, notes, "Without a doubt, both 'bad' and 'good' uses of guns occur. The question isn't really whether both occur; it is, rather, Which is more important?"[3] In one sense, Lott is simply alluding to the fact that both

> **Of the 10,100 murders committed with firearms [in 2005], 7,543 were committed with handguns.**

sides of the gun control debate have strong and valid arguments to support their views. The question is whether this serves either side particularly well.

Pro– and anti–gun control proponents do have some common goals. Neither side wants to see guns in the hands of criminals or anyone else who would use them irresponsibly. Moreover, both groups want to see accidents reduced, or even better, eliminated altogether. Despite the sometimes heated rhetoric from activists on both sides, their goals do parallel each other: safety, responsibility, and reduction of violence and crime. The real question is whether both sides can work together to achieve their goals.

Guns and children are a good case in point. People on both sides of the gun control issue believe that children are at great risk for being hurt or killed accidentally by a gun. According to the Children's Defense Fund, 2,827 children and teens died as a result of gun violence in the United States in 2003. "The deaths of thousands of children each year is morally obscene for the world's most powerful nation, which has more resources to address its social ills than any other nation,"[4] notes Children's Defense Fund president Marian Wright Edelman. Small children may find a real gun and, thinking it is a toy, point it at someone and shoot. Or they may accidentally shoot themselves. Older children, not knowledgeable enough to truly understand how guns work, may accidentally fire a weapon, often with tragic results.

Promoting Gun Safety

Groups such as the National Shooting Sports Association (NSSF) and the National Rifle Association (NRA) have developed education programs to provide children (and their parents) with information about gun safety. The U.S. Department of Justice chose NSSF to administer the Project ChildSafe program, which provides education to children and distributes gun locks free of charge. As NSSF notes, "The risk of firearms-related unintentional injuries or deaths can be reduced when firearms owners are aware of and fully understand their responsibility to handle firearms safely and store them in a secure manner."[5] In 1988 the NRA launched its Eddie Eagle program. Eddie Eagle, the mascot, helps bring the word to children from preschool to third grade that guns are not safe even to touch. The training program, which includes workbooks and videos, teaches children Eddie Eagle's message about guns: not to touch any gun they find, but to leave the area and tell an adult. Past NRA president Marion Hammer, who created Eddie Eagle, sees the program as "an NRA commitment that can benefit every child."[6]

> "The typical handgun is the most common firearm both because it is relatively easy to buy and easy to conceal."

Although some antigun groups found fault with the Eddie Eagle campaign (the Violence Policy Center referred to Eddie Eagle as "Joe Camel with feathers"[7]), the program has been recognized as a successful means of outreach, getting endorsements from the National Sheriffs' Association and the American Legion as well as recognition by a number of state governments. A program like this, claim its proponents, teaches gun safety to children and makes them more responsible around firearms as they enter adulthood. This, they believe, is a more effective way to "control" gun violence than merely restricting or banning gun ownership among law-abiding citizens.

Project Exile, a program adopted by several states that mandated criminals with guns be prosecuted under strict federal statutes, was embraced by both pro- and antigun advocates. Gun rights proponents can support this sort of program because it goes to what they see as the root problem—the criminal—without automatically restricting individuals' rights to own firearms. Gun control advocates can support it because, even though it does not remove guns from circulation, it does assist in keeping them out of the wrong hands.

> **Advocates for gun control claim that the huge number of guns in existence makes it easier for criminals to acquire them through theft.**

Such a polarizing issue as gun control often leaves advocates on both sides feeling frustrated. While it is clear that neither side will embrace the other, it is nonetheless important for both sides of the issue to be heard. Often the amount of common ground, if there is any at all, is small. That said, by keeping the channels of communication open and by having well-reasoned discussions on the issue, it is not impossible that gun control advocates and those who support gun ownership will be able to take positive steps to reduce gun violence and keep guns out of the hands of those who have no business with them.

Can Gun Control Reduce Crime?

"Our nation leads the industrialized world in firearms violence of all types because most of our violence involves handguns, which are relatively inexpensive, easy to acquire, and therefore ubiquitous."

—Josh Sugarman, *Every Handgun Is Aimed at You: The Case for Banning Handguns.* New York: New Press, 2001.

In 2005 the Federal Bureau of Investigation (FBI) reported 1,390,695 violent crimes committed in the United States. These crimes included murder, rape, armed robbery, and assault. Of those crimes, some 9 percent involved firearms. For murder alone, the percentage is much higher. Sixty-eight percent of the 14,860 murders committed in the United States in 2005 involved some sort of firearm, with handguns making up nearly three quarters of that percentage.

Despite the high figure for violent crimes in 2005, the FBI's data showed that violent crime had actually decreased somewhat since 2001. Curiously, however, gun violence as a percentage of violent crime had increased during that same period; compared with the 68 percent of all murders having been committed with guns in 2005, the figure for 2001 was 63 percent. Given this statistic, it is unclear whether gun control measures as they currently exist in the United States help reduce crime in general and gun crime in particular.

How Easy Is It to Get a Gun?

In the United States a law-abiding citizen who has no criminal past can purchase a gun with relatively little difficulty. Before the passage of the Brady Handgun Violence Prevention Act (the Brady Bill) in 1993, anyone who wanted to purchase a handgun could do so with no waiting period in 32 states. Other states each had their own waiting periods and requirements. The Brady Bill imposed a waiting period of up to 5 days on any unlicensed gun purchaser in those states that lacked their own background checks, which gave the seller time to make sure the buyer did not have a criminal record.

The Brady Bill was passed with the understanding that the five-day waiting period would be temporary until the FBI could develop a national check system. This was accomplished in November 1998 when the FBI announced the National Instant Criminal Background Check System (NICS). Under NICS, all federal firearms licensees (FFLs), or gun sellers, are required to run background checks on individuals attempting to purchase a firearm. Thirty states, five U.S. territories, and the District of Columbia all use NICS exclusively for background checks. Thirteen states have agencies acting on behalf of NICS in what they term a point-of-contact capacity; the agencies run background checks by accessing the NICS database. An additional eight states have agencies that act as partial points of contact; their agencies handle handgun checks while NICS handles long gun (rifles, for example) checks.

> In the United States, a law-abiding citizen who has no criminal past can purchase a gun with relatively little difficulty.

NICS runs names through a background check to ensure that the purchaser does not have a criminal record. Not every state uses NICS, and depending on the state, there may be virtually no waiting period. In some states, a permit is required to carry a gun; some states, such as Illinois, New Jersey, and North Carolina, require a wait of up to 30 days before a permit can be issued. In New York the wait can be up to 6 months. Other states that do not follow the NICS program have waiting periods of anything from 2 to 14 days.

Who Cannot Get a Gun?

NICS is designed to identify people who are ineligible to purchase or acquire firearms. The list is comprehensive. Anyone convicted of a felony that includes a sentence of more than 1 year (or a misdemeanor if the sentence exceeds 2 years) cannot purchase a firearm, even if no sentence is actually imposed. Those who have been convicted of using certain controlled substances, such as narcotics, cannot purchase firearms. Nor can anyone who has renounced his or her United States citizenship. Illegal aliens cannot purchase firearms. Anyone who has been dishonorably discharged from the U.S. military cannot purchase a firearm. Those who have orders of protection against them (for example, those accused of spouse abuse) or who have been convicted of violence against a spouse or child cannot purchase firearms. No one who is deemed mentally incapable of handling his or her own affairs can purchase a firearm. As of 2005 some 3.9 million people were listed as ineligible in the NICS system. The FBI's figures show that between 1998 and 2005, nearly 60 million background checks were conducted and 450,000 people had been denied the purchase of firearms.

> **One of the most problematic features of NICS is a loophole that requires background checks to be completed within 3 days. After that, the gun dealer is allowed to turn the gun over to the purchaser by default.**

One of the most problematic features of NICS is a loophole that requires background checks to be completed within three days. After that, the gun dealer is allowed to turn the gun over to the purchaser by default. According to the U.S. General Accounting Office, that loophole resulted in 10,945 "prohibited purchasers" being sold guns between November 1998 and September 2001.

How Criminals Acquire Guns

People who are listed as ineligible for purchasing guns can get them in other ways. They can get them on the black market. "Black market" is a term used to cover a wide array of illegal transactions. People buy and sell all kinds of items illegally on the black market. The black market is an easy place to obtain guns, and there are plenty to choose from.

While estimates vary as to how many guns are purchased through the black market, the Center for Gun Policy and Research at Johns Hopkins University estimates that some 500,000 guns are stolen from gun owners each year. Many of those guns are sold to individuals who could not buy guns legally.

Illegal gun sales also take place through straw purchases. In a straw purchase, a person who has no criminal record makes the purchase for someone who does have a record. (A person who engages in such a purchase is committing a felony.) In addition to allowing criminals to get hold of guns, straw purchases are problematic because they give law enforcement officials no easy way to track these weapons to the people who are actually using them.

Benefits of Waiting and Background Checking

John Hinckley, the man who shot President Ronald Reagan and White House press secretary James Brady in March 1981, purchased his gun on the spot after he wrote a phony address on his application form. With no mandatory background checking system in place, there was no way to find out that Hinckley had provided false information. Today, Hinckley's application would have been flagged and his purchase denied.

Waiting periods can also serve another purpose: They can delay gun purchases. A delay can be a good thing when the person buying the gun is buying it out of anger. Domestic violence shootings—when an angry spouse shoots his or her spouse or estranged spouse—are a good example. According to the FBI,

> **The black market is an easy place to obtain guns, and there are plenty to choose from.**

33 percent of all women murdered with guns are killed by an intimate partner—and households that have firearms are eight times more likely to experience domestic violence–related shootings. Guns purchased by angry employees or by suicidal individuals fall into this category as well. A waiting period can act as a "cooling-off" period—which can give an angry spouse or an unhappy worker a chance to reconsider committing a rash and irreversible action.

Gaps in the System

Although background checks and waiting periods can prevent gun violence, they do not always succeed. A person who is determined to buy a gun can usually find a way around the system. This is where waiting periods and background checks fall short—not because of their own inherent flaws but because the system itself has gaps.

This is what happened in the case of Eric Harris and Dylan Klebold, the two teenagers who walked into Littleton, Colorado's Columbine High School on April 20, 1999, and killed 12 classmates, a teacher, and themselves. They were not old enough to purchase the weapons they used that day. They found a person who agreed to make a straw purchase for them for some of the weapons; another person sold them more weapons even though he knew he was selling to minors.

There were background checks and laws against selling firearms to minors in effect in Colorado when Harris and Klebold began to accumulate their store of weapons. But even if no background checks had existed in Colorado, no legitimate gun dealer would have sold weapons to two minors (a crime under federal law). The teenagers knew this and found a way to get the weapons they wanted anyway. They were able to completely bypass the system of checks and balances that the federal government had set up to prevent just such tragedies.

> **Households that have firearms are eight times more likely to experience domestic violence–related shootings.**

James Brady, for whom the Brady Bill is named, says that this is a critical problem that must be addressed comprehensively. On the 25th anniversary of his shooting (along with the assassination attempt on President Ronald Reagan), Brady noted, "Twenty-five years after a deeply disturbed individual came within an inch of killing the leader of the free world, it is still far too easy for criminals to buy all the guns they want."[8]

In 2001 U.S. representative Henry Waxman, ranking minority member of the House Committee on Government Reform, asked the General Accounting Office (GAO) to track how well gun dealers are regulated under NICS. What the GAO found was that it was relatively simple for unscrupulous individuals to forge a gun dealer license and use it to have access to firearms for sale or transfer. (Gun dealers can sell to each other without undergoing background checks.) The findings, Waxman wrote in a letter to Treasury Secretary Paul O'Neill in April 2002, "depict a regulatory scheme in which criminals can forge gun dealer licenses easily, bypass background checks, and buy multiple guns for use in criminal activity."[9]

Gun rights advocates believe that this is a key element of the problem: People who are intent on acquiring guns to commit crimes will do so regardless of restrictions. As syndicated columnist Charley Reese notes, "Criminals are by definition lawbreakers and don't obey gun-control laws."[10]

What the Figures Say

Do the statistics show that restrictions on purchasing guns have a measurable impact on the amount of gun crime in the United States? As with most statistics, especially when it comes to guns, different groups evaluate them differently. A report released in 2003 by the Centers for Disease Control and Prevention (CDC) analyzed 51 separate studies. The analysis found some evidence that gun control can be useful but also noted that in general, the information on this topic is insufficient to draw definitive conclusions, and more research is needed.

Gun rights proponents touted this study as supportive of the position that restrictions on firearms have no noticeable effect on violent crime. The National Rifle Association (NRA), in fact, has cited other studies that support this view. For example, the NRA's Institute for Legislative Action has reported that Washington, D.C., which banned handguns in 1976, had seen its murder rate triple by 1991 while for the same period the national murder rate rose only 12 percent. It also cited the example of California: After California imposed a 15-day waiting period for gun purchases in 1975, its violent crime rate rose 50 percent each year. (The waiting period was reduced to 10 days in 1997.)

Gun control advocates saw another message in the CDC's figures. Shortly after the CDC report was released, the Legal Community Against Violence (LCAV), a national clearinghouse for legal information and efforts to strengthen gun laws, did its own analysis of the CDC numbers. The LCAV concluded that the CDC report demonstrated that "our country's gun laws have had a positive impact."[11] The LCAV also cited other studies to bolster its case. For example, a 1999 study found that the federal assault weapons ban (the same one that was allowed to sunset in 2004) had reduced criminal use of assault weapons by 20 percent. And, the LCAV said, laws restricting gun purchases in Virginia, Maryland, and other states had likewise reduced gun-related crime. The conclusion that the LCAV reached was that the CDC's findings did not disprove in any way the effectiveness of gun control legislation or action.

The Debate Continues

There may be difficulty in finding common ground between gun control advocates and opponents when it comes to the role of guns in criminal activity. One thing is clear: There will always be people who misuse firearms and who commit violent crimes by wielding weapons. Whether the solution is to restrict guns and ammunition, to enforce current anticrime laws more consistently, or a combination of both, the debate is sure to continue.

Primary Source Quotes*

Can Gun Control Reduce Crime?

"Unless governments act to stop the spread of arms, deadly weapons will continue to fuel violent conflict, state repression, crime, and domestic abuse."

—Jeremy Hobbs, Oxfam press release, June 19, 2006. www.oxfam.org.

Hobbs is the international director of Oxfam, a human rights group that works to find solutions to poverty and injustice.

"President Clinton has fought hard for every kind of firearm restriction imaginable. Yet at the same time he has, as a matter of policy, refused to vigorously enforce federal gun laws already on the books."

—Charlton Heston, speech delivered at Georgetown University, March 29, 2000. www.alum.dartmouth.org.

Heston is an actor and former NRA president.

* Editor's Note: While the definition of a primary source can be narrowly or broadly defined, for the purposes of Compact Research, a primary source consists of: 1) results of original research presented by an organization or researcher; 2) eyewitness accounts of events, personal experience, or work experience; 3) first-person editorials offering pundits' opinions; 4) government officials presenting political plans and/or policies; 5) representatives of organizations presenting testimony or policy.

Primary Source Quotes

❝I think there are lots of people who have handguns and really are fairly unstable, and I think the laws have made it fairly easy for those people to have handguns.**❞**

—Josh Sugarman, *Every Handgun Is Aimed at You: The Case for Banning Handguns.* New York: New Press, 2001.

Sugarman is executive director of the Violence Policy Center.

❝The government has neither the obligation nor the ability to offer its citizens reliable protection from murder, rape, and robbery. The police almost always arrive at the scene of a crime well after the crime has been committed, and no one would want to have police officers stationed everywhere that crime might occur.**❞**

—Nelson Lund, "Taking the Second Amendment Seriously," *Weekly Standard,* July 24, 2000.

Lund is a professor at the George Mason University School of Law.

❝[Because of the Brady Bill] 500,000 people have been kept from getting handguns because they were felons, fugitives, and stalkers.**❞**

—President Bill Clinton, speech before the Democratic National Committee, March 15, 2000. www.findarticles.com.

Clinton is the 42nd president of the United States.

❝In 1994, we passed a crime bill to put 100,000 cops on the street and take assault weapons off. Now, in 2004, this president has moved to take those cops off the street and has stood by as the assault weapons ban expires.❞

—Dianne Feinstein, remarking on the sunset provision of the federal assault weapons ban in a statement delivered on September 13, 2004. http://feinstein.senate.gov.

Feinstein is a Democratic U.S. senator from California.

❝Voluntary firearms safety training, not government intrusion, has decreased firearms accidents.❞

—National Rifle Association, Institute for Legislative Action, fact sheet, October 16, 2006. www.nraila.org.

The NRA's Institute for Legislative Action works with legislators to ensure that gun owners' rights are protected.

❝There are millions of Americans out there who never hear anything but arguments against gun ownership.❞

—Bernard Goldberg, *Arrogance: Rescuing America from the Media Elite.* New York: Warner, 2003.

Goldberg is a media journalist and author of several books on the media.

❝Most criminals are not the fearless supermen portrayed in films such as Predator II. . . . By and large they are cowards who prey on women and old people, seeking to avoid a fair fight at all costs. . . . In 98 percent of the reported cases, criminals flee the moment they realize their intended victim is armed.❞

—Richard Poe, *The Seven Myths of Gun Control.* New York: Forum, 2001.

Poe is a journalist and author.

66 The ban has been in effect for nearly a decade, and not one hunter has lost his right to hunt, not one home-owner has lost his power to defend his home. We have proven that the Second Amendment can thrive while we take limited and reasonable measures to protect Americans from gun violence. 99

> — Charles Schumer, remarks about the Assault Weapons Ban's success (in anticipation of a renewal battle), May 8, 2003. http://schumer.senate.gov.

Schumer, a U.S. senator (D-NY), is one of the most active gun control–supporting legislators in Congress.

66 I believe law-abiding citizens ought to be able to own a gun. I believe in background checks. The best way to protect our citizens from guns is to prosecute those who commit crimes with guns. 99

> —George W. Bush, presidential debate with Senator John Kerry in Tempe, Arizona, OnTheIssues, October 13, 2004. www.issues2000.org.

Bush is the 43rd president of the United States.

66 The biggest problem with gun control laws is that those who are intent on harming others . . . are the least likely to obey them. 99

> —John R. Lott Jr., *More Guns, Less Crime.* Chicago: University of Chicago Press, 2000.

Lott is a law professor and senior research scholar at Yale Law School.

Can Gun Control Reduce Crime?

- According to the Bureau of Justice Statistics, in 2005 more than 70 percent of all homicides were committed with firearms.

- An October 2004 report by the Americans for Gun Safety Foundation (AGSF) found that 20 of the 22 major federal gun laws are enforced so infrequently that they might as well not exist.

- The Australian government banned firearms in 1996 after a well-publicized shooting. Immediately after the ban, according to a 2000 report by the Australian Bureau of Statistics, armed robberies rose by 73 percent, unarmed robberies by 28 percent, kidnappings by 38 percent, assaults by 17 percent, and manslaughter by 29 percent.

- In the first 3 months of 2004, the FBI received 1,129,588 calls from stores checking to make sure individuals were eligible to purchase a gun. Of those, 15,794 were turned down.

- The National Crime Victimization Survey (Bureau of Justice Statistics) found that between 1993 and 2001 nearly 26 percent of all violent crimes (annual average 8.9 million) were committed with a weapon.

- In 2005, according to the FBI, there were 192 "justifiable homicides" in the United States. This involves, for example, private citizens who kill a criminal in the act of committing a felony. Of those homicides, 143 were with a gun (119 handguns, 5 rifles, 6 shotguns).

Nonfatal Gun-Related Violent Crime

This graph shows how nonfatal gun-related violent crime has declined over 73 percent from 1994 to 2004. This sharp decline has been largely attributable to the passing of the Brady Handgun Act in November 1993. Violent crime includes rape, sexual assault, robbery, and aggravated assault.

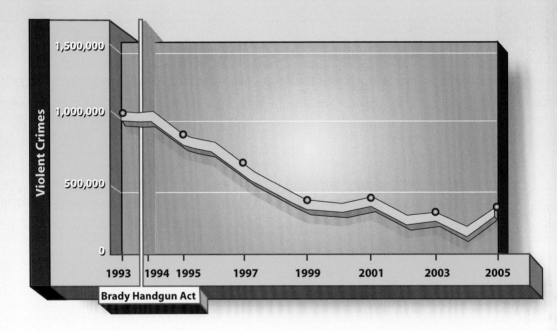

Source: FBI's Uniform Crime Reports, "National Crime Victimization Survey," 2006. www.ojp.usdoj.gov.

- The Coalition to Stop Gun Violence estimated in 2003 that some 40 percent of gun sales in the United States take place without a background check.

- According to the Americans for Gun Safety Foundation (AGSF), in 2003 the U.S. Justice Department brought only 188 cases for gun trafficking to trial despite the recovery of 300,000 guns showing signs of trafficking. This represents a 5 percent decline in prosecutions from 2002 levels.

• According to the Coalition to Stop Gun Violence, 40 percent of all gun sales are made through the secondary market (when a legal purchaser sells to someone else privately, either legally or illegally), where background checks are not required. This has the potential to allow criminals to bypass the system entirely.

Violent Crime Rates Decline After Brady Handgun Act

This chart shows how violent crime has dropped dramatically since the passing of the Brady Handgun Act in November of 1993. The drop in violent crime parallels the decline in gun-related crime. Violent crime includes rape, robbery, aggravated assault, and homicide.

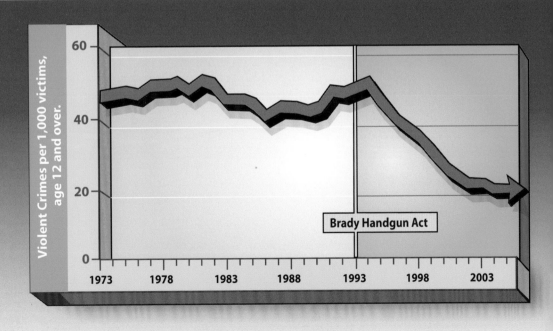

Source: FBI's uniform Crime Reports, "National Crime Victimization Survey," 2006. www.oip.usdoj.gov.

- According to the Americans for Gun Safety Foundation, in 2003, 87 percent of all prosecutions under federal firearms laws involved two statutes—the provisions covering felons in possession of guns and the use of a gun in the commission of a violent felony or drug crime.

Firearm Murders

This chart shows how many murders were caused by firearms from 2001 to 2005. The number of firearm murders increased 14 percent from 2001 to 2005. Handguns account for over 75 percent of all gun-related murders.

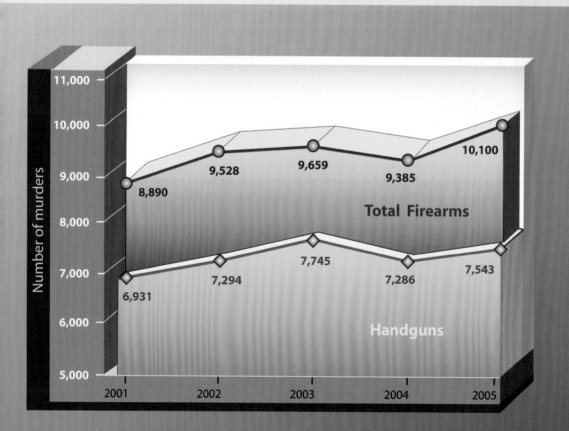

Source: Federal Bureau of Investigation, "Crime in the United States," 2005. www.fbi.gov.

How Americans Feel About Laws Governing Firearm Sales

According to this ongoing survey, since 1993, the year the Brady Handgun Act was passed, fewer Americans feel that laws regulating the sale of guns should be stricter. This indicates that many people were satisfied with the impact of the Brady Bill, which required background checks and waiting periods to purchase a handgun.

In general, do you feel that the laws covering the sale of firearms should be made more strict, less strict, or kept as they are now?

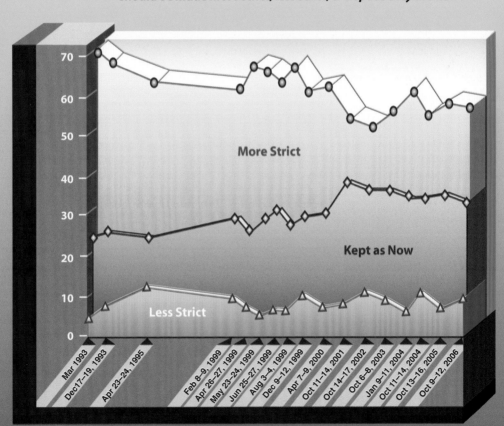

Source: The Gallup Poll, "Gun Laws." www.galluppoll.com.

Could Gun Control Reduce Youth Violence?

66 **What does it take for a kid to buy a $50 handgun? About $50. And the underground market. And weak gun restrictions. And slack enforcement.** 99

—Children's Defense Fund, advertising campaign for anti–gun violence program.

The role of firearms in the lives of young people is often a grim one. Incidents happen, too regularly, in which disturbed adolescents come to school armed with guns and shoot classmates and teachers (often killing themselves afterwards). The steady rise of gang violence, not only in the inner cities but also in suburban neighborhoods, almost always means that youths have access to guns. For much younger children, there are tragic stories of five-year-olds who shoot a friend or sibling while playing with what they think is a toy gun.

Incidences of accidental deaths and injuries, fatalities resulting from criminal activity, and children who are shot as innocent bystanders during gang violence or domestic abuse are alarmingly high. A study conducted by the Children's Defense Fund and released in June 2006 revealed that in 2003 there were 2,827 gun deaths among children and teens in the United States. This is more than the number of American troops killed by hostile fire during the first 3 years of the Iraq War. The study also noted that the number of children who were wounded but not killed by gunfire was as high as 5 times the number of children who were killed.

Advocates for children take the issue of gun-related deaths and injuries seriously. In 2004 a group including the Ambulatory Pediatric Association, the American Academy of Pediatrics, the American Association for the Surgery of Trauma, the American College of Emergency Physicians, and the American Public Health Association released a statement asking political candidates from both parties to take the issue of gun violence toward children seriously: "There is great irony in the fact that US policy is currently consumed by efforts to deal with small arms violence abroad, yet appears to ignore it at home."[12]

How Do Kids Get Guns?

Federal law prohibits anyone under 18 from possessing guns and anyone under 21 from purchasing guns from licensed dealers. State laws, however, vary in this regard; many states allow minors to possess rifles but not handguns, and some states allow minors to purchase guns from private dealers. The Brady Center to Prevent Gun Violence publishes an annual state-by-state child firearm safety "report card" that tracks which states have restrictions on gun sales or possession by minors, parental permission or notification when a child acquires a gun, and safety measures such as childproof caps on guns. The 2005 report card gave 32 states a grade of D or F. (No state received a grade of A; only 7 states—California, Connecticut, Hawaii, Illinois, Maryland, Massachusetts, and New Jersey—received a grade of A-.) This means that although federal law keeps a 16-year-old from buying handguns from licensed dealers, in some states that same 16-year-old may purchase a rifle from a private dealer and use it to hunt on his own property.

> The steady rise of gang violence . . . almost always means that youths have access to guns.

Even with laws prohibiting sale and possession by minors, teenagers can still get hold of guns if they want to. Dylan Klebold and Eric Harris, the teenagers who carried out the Columbine High School massacre in Littleton, Colorado, in April 1999, obtained their guns through illegal sources with no difficulty.

Minors can obtain guns through the black market (illegal sales of illegal weapons). Teenagers who have the cash and who can make a connection to a black market dealer can purchase any firearm. They can also purchase firearms through straw purchases (in which a person with no criminal background purchases a gun for someone else).

Many youths simply find guns at home if their parents hunt, shoot for sport, or collect guns. Ostensibly gun owners keep their guns and ammunition locked up, but often this is not the case. This is how small children often get hold of firearms and accidentally fire them, frequently with tragic results. Sometimes, otherwise responsible adults may leave their guns unlocked—perhaps because they feel comfortable that their children do understand gun safety. Notes Jim McVay, director of the Bureau of Health Promotion and Chronic Disease in Alabama's Department of Public Health, "We have a hunting tradition in the Deep South, but there is no excuse for having loaded guns in the house."[13] Even if guns are kept locked away, teenagers who are suicidal or homicidal will likely be able to break into locked cabinets.

> "A study conducted by the Children's Defense Fund and released in June 2006 revealed that in 2003 there were 2,827 gun deaths among children and teens in the United States."

Child Access Prevention Laws

Nineteen states have laws or regulations that hold gun owners accountable if they leave a firearm within easy access of a child. These Child Access Prevention (CAP) laws are designed to compel gun owners to make sure their guns and ammunition are securely stored and not within easy reach of minors. If a minor breaks into a securely locked cabinet or container and steals a gun and ammunition, the gun owner is not liable. Gun owners can also avoid being held liable if their guns are equipped with child safety locks that render the gun unable to be fired by anyone who cannot remove the lock.

Florida enacted CAP legislation in 1989 in response to a rising number of gun fatalities among children. The legislation appeared to have a profound and quick impact; according to the National Center for Health Statistics, the number of unintentional shootings in Florida fell by more than 50 percent in the year after the law went into effect. Several cities, including Houston, Baltimore, and Wichita, also have CAP laws. Those found guilty of violating the law are subject to fines or imprisonment.

Gun ownership proponents are generally not in favor of CAP laws, in part because they believe it could jeopardize a gun owner's ability to use his or her weapon in self-defense. They also feel that CAP laws are merely a quick fix to a more pressing problem—teaching gun safety. If children learned proper gun safety techniques, they would not play with loaded firearms. "Gun control supporters advocate government intrusion, rather than education, to reduce accidents,"[14] says the NRA. While this may be true, say gun control advocates, it is unrealistic to expect all children to be well versed in gun safety, especially very small children who may not understand the concept. Moreover, most child safety locks are easily removed by the gun owner in a matter of seconds. This should allow use of the gun if needed—even in an emergency.

Gangs and Gun Violence

Youth gangs present a particularly difficult challenge, especially in large cities. The National Youth Gang Center (NYGC), part of the U.S. Department of Justice's Office of Juvenile Justice and Delinquency Prevention, reports that for cities or communities of fewer than 50,000 residents, gang activity is cyclical and is generally not a hugely significant problem. But in cities of more than 100,000, and especially in very large cities, gangs can present a huge problem. The NYGC reports that large cities may typically be home to some 30 gangs made up of more than 1,000 gang members. Nationwide the number of gang members is estimated at approximately 750,000. Nearly 40 percent of them are under 18.

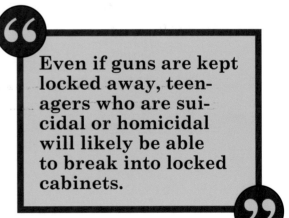

Even if guns are kept locked away, teenagers who are suicidal or homicidal will likely be able to break into locked cabinets.

With gangs come criminal activity, often in the form of violent crime. Gangs are responsible for assaults and robberies, as well as murders (of rival gang members but also within the general public). The NYGC reported that in Los Angeles and Chicago (both with a heavy gang presence) in 2004, more than half of the 1,000 combined homicides in both cities were gang related. In 171 other large cities surveyed, about a quarter of their homicides were considered gang related. Many of these homicides were committed with guns.

Gang members, like other criminals, have relatively easy access to firearms; either they steal them or they obtain them through the black market. They use them in the commission of crimes, and they also bring them to school. According to NYGC statistics, communities that have gang activity are 25 percent more likely to find guns in the schools, despite the efforts of many school districts to screen out firearms (with guards and metal detectors).

Gun control advocates believe that curtailing the number of available guns could reduce gang violence because they would no longer have easy access to guns. Gun rights proponents counter that gang members will always find a way to steal weapons, and stricter gun control laws such as more careful licensing or waiting periods would not affect gang members.

According to NYGC statistics, communities that have gang activity are 25 percent more likely to find guns in the schools.

Several states have enacted legislation to deal with gun violence involving gangs. In Louisiana, Mississippi, and Missouri, for example, firearms can be confiscated if they are believed to be used for gang-related crime. And Arizona, Georgia, and Idaho provide special penalties for those who supply firearms to gang members.

Tackling Gun Violence Through Outreach

Over the years, several initiatives involving federal, state, and local resources have been implemented to serve as an adjunct to traditional gun control. One example is the Youth Crime Gun Interdiction Initiative (YCGII), a program that allows federal, state, and local law enforcement officials to join forces to reduce gun violence among youths. In its first year, 27 cities participated in the program, which, among other achievements, significantly helped in the tracing of guns involved in crimes and the collection of data about illegal guns. In 2005 the program was folded into the Bush administration's Project Safe Neighborhoods.

Another example is Boston's Operation Cease Fire, a task force composed of federal, state, and local law enforcement officials. Called the "Boston Miracle," the

> " **Gun owners groups are . . . involved in gun safety programs for youth.** "

program reached out into communities that were particularly hard-hit by gun violence. Members of the task force met with community leaders and gang members, explaining that juveniles engaging in violent crimes or behavior would be subject to sustained intensive police action until the violence stopped. Repeat offenders were prosecuted to the fullest extent of the law. While not "gun control" in its typical form, the program helped reduce gun violence by getting criminals (and some guns) off the streets.

Project Safe Neighborhoods (PSN), created in the spring of 2001, is a collaboration between the U.S. attorney in each of the nation's 94 federal judicial districts and local law enforcement officials and community leaders. The goal is to ensure that current criminal penalties for gun possession and gun crimes are strictly enforced as a means of punishing criminals and deterring would-be criminals. Again, while not gun control per se, it does help get violent criminals off the streets. Gun ownership advocates believe this is the real way to thwart gun violence—prosecuting criminals and keeping them from harming others.

Initiatives from the Pro-Gun Side

Gun owners groups are also involved in gun safety programs for youth. The NRA and the National Shooting Sports Foundation (NSSF) have for years offered training programs for youths and adults, with the belief that youths who understand the rules of gun safety will respect guns more and will be less likely to have shooting accidents. The NRA has geared part of its efforts in this regard toward younger children through the Eddie Eagle campaign. The Eddie Eagle program, which began in 1988, teaches gun safety to children from preschool to third grade. It teaches gun safety through a series of workbooks and exercises and an animated video—along with Eddie Eagle, the program's mascot. Launched in 1988, by 2005 it had reached some 17 million children in the United States and Canada.

Gun control advocates claim that efforts like Eddie Eagle, while not harmful, have little positive impact on reducing gun violence. The safety training may help some children stay away from guns, they say, but the continued availability of guns still puts young people at risk.

An issue as emotional as guns and youth elicits strong responses on both sides of the gun control issue. Both sides make valid points; more gun safety training will certainly result in the safer handling of guns, but the availability of firearms means that troubled youths and gang members can still get hold of guns and wreak havoc with them. The complexity of this particular gun control topic makes it hard to offer up simple answers, and it is clear that it will continue to be a difficult point for both sides.

Primary Source Quotes*

Could Gun Control Reduce Youth Violence?

❝The safest thing for your family is not to keep a gun in the home.❞

—American Academy of Pediatrics, Child Health Month fact sheet, 2006. www.aap.org.

The American Academy of Pediatrics is an organization of pediatricians who are committed to the physical and emotional well-being of children.

....

❝The grip of gun-control hysteria has even led one New Jersey nursery school to expel four toddlers for simply pretending to shoot guns with their index fingers.❞

—Michelle Malkin, "In Defense of an Armed Citizenry," *Jewish World Review,* April 13, 2000.

Malkin is a political writer and syndicated columnist.

....

* Editor's Note: While the definition of a primary source can be narrowly or broadly defined, for the purposes of Compact Research, a primary source consists of: 1) results of original research presented by an organization or researcher; 2) eyewitness accounts of events, personal experience, or work experience; 3) first-person editorials offering pundits' opinions; 4) government officials presenting political plans and/or policies; 5) representatives of organizations presenting testimony or policy.

66 **Although young people are closely involved with the problem of gun violence they are rarely consulted as part of the solution. Traditionally they have not been invited to participate in discussions on the topic either at the regional or international level.** 99

—Joseph Dube, "Young People Are Part of the Solution on Gun Violence." www.iansa.org.

Dube is campaign coordinator for the International Action Network on Small Arms (IANSA).

66 **If toaster ovens were killing kids in the home, we wouldn't have toaster ovens. . . . But still there are guns.** 99

—Jonathan I. Groner, quoted in the *Columbus (OH) Dispatch*, February 6, 2000.

Groner, a surgeon, has conducted research into gun deaths and children.

66 **Reports of one school shooting can disturb children and teachers in classrooms around the country. Children can't learn if they're worried about their safety, which is why adults must do everything they can to reassure children through their own actions.** 99

—Laura Bush, speaking at a conference on school safety at the National 4-H Youth Conference Center, Chevy Chase, Maryland , October 10, 2006. www.whitehouse.gov.

Bush is the First Lady of the United States.

66 **Experiencing the consequences of gun violence at an early age can be . . . a key reason as to why some children come to view guns as legitimate tools for conflict resolution.** 99

—International Action Network on Small Arms (IANSA), "Small Arms and Children," fact sheet, 2006. www.iansa.org.

IANSA is an organization that works to reduce gun violence and gun proliferation around the world.

66When a fatherless kid in a crackhouse finds a stolen gun and shoots a schoolmate, stand up and say giving drug dealers triggerlocks isn't a solution.99

—Charlton Heston, speech at Brandeis University, March 28, 2000. www.nrahq.org.

Heston is an Academy Award–winning actor and former president of the National Rifle Association.

66Avoid at all cost the possession of a lethal weapon, the use of which will likely ruin your life. You are the future of this city. Lay down your weapons. Do it now.99

—John Street, "Mayor Street's Plea to Youth," *Philadelphia Inquirer,* July 30, 2006.

Street is the mayor of Philadelphia, Pennsylvania.

66Children are playful and active. Adolescents are curious and impulsive. Such healthy traits when mixed with guns can cause death. The best way to protect children against gun violence is to remove all guns from the home.99

—American Academy for Child and Adolescent Psychiatry (AACAP), "Facts for Families," July 2004. http://aacap.org.

AACAP is a professional organization of physicians who deal with children and adolescents who suffer from mental, developmental, and behavioral disorders.

Facts and Illustrations

Could Gun Control Reduce Youth Violence?

- A parent or guardian may purchase firearms and ammunition for a minor but must provide written permission for the minor to use the gun and only for specific purposes (ranching, farming, hunting).

- In the 2000 National Youth Gang Survey (NYGS), 84 percent of the jurisdictions that reported gang problems had at least one occurrence of firearm use by one or more gang members in an assault crime.

- In 2003, according the Centers for Disease Control and Prevention, 5,570 youths aged 10 to 24 were murdered (15 per day). Of those murders, 82 percent were committed with firearms.

- In 2002, according to the Children's Defense Fund, 56 law enforcement officers were killed in the line of duty; for the same period, 71 children under the age of five were killed by firearms.

- According to a survey of gun owners who had children aged 5 to 15 at home, only 12 percent of those owners kept their firearms locked and unloaded.

- Among youths aged 10 to 19, only motor vehicle accidents are responsible for more deaths than firearms.

- In 2002, nearly 1.7 million children under the age of 18 lived in homes with firearms that are both loaded and unlocked, according to a study conducted by the American Academy of Pediatrics.

- According to a 2006 survey conducted for PAX, a nonprofit organization dedicated to eliminating gun violence, 78 percent of parents would be concerned if they knew there was a gun where their child played, and 97 percent of parents who owned a gun said they would not feel uncomfortable if asked about the presence of a gun in their home by another parent.

Juvenile Arrest Rate for Weapons Violations (Aged 10–17)

The juvenile arrest rate for weapons offenses more than doubled from 1981 to 1993; however, the rate dropped over 50 percent from 1993 to 2002 reflecting the impact of the Brady Handgun Act that was passed in late November 1993.

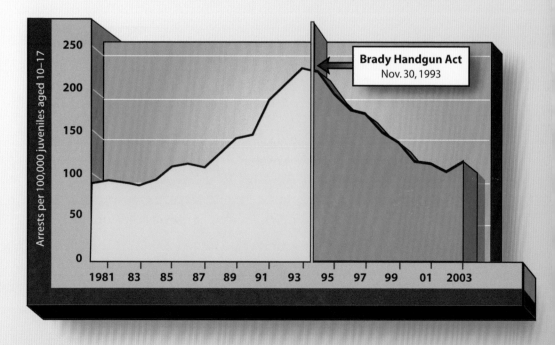

Source: U.S. Department of Justice, "Juvenile Offenders and Victims: 2006 National Report," 2006.

- The Consumer Product Safety Commission reported in 2001 that all but 2 of 32 trigger locks it tested could be easily defeated. California is the only state that has set strict standards for these locks.

- According to a 2001 study published in the *Archives of Pediatrics and Adolescent Medicine*, among inner-city 7-year-olds, 75 percent reported having heard gunshots.

- According to the National Youth Gang Survey, in 2004 nearly 1 quarter of all homicides in 171 cities with populations above 100,000

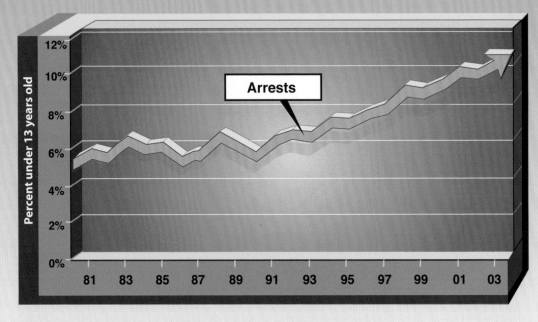

Rate of Youths (Under 13) Arrested for Weapons Increasing

Between 1981 and 2003 the arrest rate for youths under 13 for possession of weapons increased. By 2003 almost 12 percent of youths had been arrested for weapons possession.

Source: U.S. Department of Justice, "Juvenile Offenders and Victims: 2006 National Report," 2006.

Teenagers and Guns

Are there guns in your home?

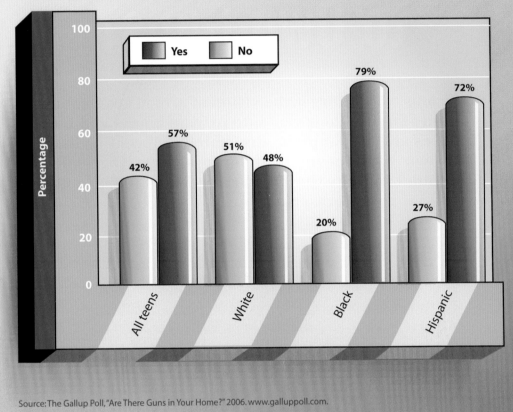

Source: The Gallup Poll, "Are There Guns in Your Home?" 2006. www.galluppoll.com.

(excluding Los Angeles and Chicago) were considered to be gang-related. In Los Angeles and Chicago, more than half of the nearly 1,000 homicides were considered gang-related.

- Project ChildSafe, funded in part through grants from the U.S. Department of Justice and administered by the National Shooting Sports Foundation, has distributed more than 35 million child safety locks throughout the United States since 2003.

Does the Constitution Guarantee the Right to Own Guns?

> **"** We must never forget the vision of armed government agents forcing their way into private homes and businesses and, at gunpoint, disarming innocent civilians of their only means of defense against the violent criminal anarchy that filled the vacuum left by a nonexistent police presence. **"**
>
> —Wayne LaPierre, NRA executive vice president and CEO, discussing New Orleans after Hurricane Katrina, 2006.

The Second Amendment of the U.S. Constitution states, "A well regulated Militia, being necessary to the security of a free State, the right of the people to keep and bear Arms, shall not be infringed." Exactly what do these 27 words mean? To some, they mean that only militias should be allowed unrestricted access to guns; to others, it means that all Americans have the right to own guns.

The framers of the Constitution have long been praised for using language that allowed adjustments for modern life while still clearly stating enduring principles. Yet the Second Amendment has left people on both sides of the gun debate wondering who should have a right to own guns and how far that right should be taken.

Original Intent of the Second Amendment

The origins of what became the Second Amendment have been traced by some historians to laws laid out by the Saxons (a Germanic tribe) after they had invaded Britain beginning in the sixth century. The Saxons

50

stipulated that all healthy free men had a duty to bear arms in the service of protecting their people and that landowners had to maintain armor and weapons for use by troops during invasions.

Chances are that the framers of the U.S. Constitution knew something about Saxon laws, but more likely their model was England's Declaration of Rights. This document, written in 1688, guaranteed Englishmen certain basic rights, including the right to bear arms. Although the government of the United States was very different from that of England, much of the basic structure of the Constitution reflects English influence.

After the United States declared its independence from Great Britain, its goal in forming a national government was to create one that would not infringe on the basic rights of its citizens. The Bill of Rights, the first 10 amendments to the U.S. Constitution, grew out of this goal. The right of individuals to bear arms as a means of self-defense and self-preservation was considered just as important a right as freedom of speech and freedom of religion. In fact, it is believed, based on his earlier drafts, that James Madison, who largely wrote the Bill of Rights, considered the right to bear arms as much more of an individual right than the language of the final bill indicated.

> **The framers of the Constitution have long been praised for using language that allowed adjustments for modern life while still clearly stating enduring principles.**

At the time the Constitution was written the United States was a very different place from what it is today. Americans in the 1780s, except perhaps those in the larger cities, had to contend with wild animals, Native Americans who had been displaced from their land, and fugitives from justice. Because standing armies as we know them today did not exist, (the first military draft took place during the Civil War in 1861), the issue of protection of home and family was essentially left to individuals.

Moreover, until the Industrial Revolution of the 19th century caused people to migrate toward large urban centers, America was primarily an agricultural country. People produced their own food and what they did not produce, they hunted. Hunting at that time was for many a necessity, not a sport. Thus, owning a gun was not merely a means of protection. For many it was also a means of day-to-day survival.

The Second Amendment in Modern Times

Not surprisingly, both sides of the gun control issue have a different interpretation of exactly what the Second Amendment means today. The Second Amendment Foundation (SAF), an educational and legal rights group for those who favor gun ownership, reads the Second Amendment (and in fact all the amendments that make up the Bill of Rights) to mean that individual Americans should be protected from an overreaching federal government. State governments, likewise, should be protected; each sovereign state should be able to chart its own course with minimal interference from federal powers. Of the Second Amendment specifically, the SAF believes that it guarantees law-abiding adult Americans the right to defend themselves: "We believe that the Second Amendment right to self-protection and defense of liberty should be granted to all those eligible, including everyone of legal age and those who are not violent criminals."[15]

> **The right of individuals to bear arms as a means of self-defense and self-preservation was considered just as important a right as freedom of speech and freedom of religion.**

What Is the Militia?

What exactly is the militia as outlined in the Second Amendment? At the time the Constitution was ratified, the militia generally consisted of able-bodied male citizens aged 17 to 45. Others, including women, the elderly, and even children, could in theory be called upon to serve as a "reserve" militia.

The Brady Campaign to Prevent Gun Violence notes that each state was essentially responsible for its own defense. Thus, each individual state had its own active militia, consisting of ordinary citizens who served as soldiers part-time. Those part-time soldiers received training but supplied their own firearms. "[The militia] was a form of compulsory military service intended to protect the fledgling nation from outside forces and from internal rebellions."[16]

Gun control advocates see the militia, as outlined in the Second Amendment, as similar to today's National Guard. That means only those who are trained and serving in such a group would require access to firearms and ammunition. Gun rights advocates, however, include the reserve militia in the definition and believe that the Second Amendment means *all* American citizens have a right to bear arms.

Responsible Gun Ownership

Gun control advocates, who see no connection between the Second Amendment and individual gun ownership, believe that no individual has a constitutionally guaranteed right to own firearms. Gun rights advocates, who read the Second Amendment as though its original intent still stands today, believe that no law-abiding citizen's right to own a gun should be infringed upon.

Hunters and target shooters are among the largest and most prolific gun owners in the United States. According to the National Shooting Sports Foundation (NSSF), there are 18.5 million hunters in the U.S., and hunting is a $30 billion industry employing 986,000 people across the country. There are also approximately 19 million target shooters in the United States, and target shooting is a popular hobby worldwide. In addition, groups such as NSSF and the National Rifle Association (NRA) provide comprehensive safety training in the form of instruction and videos. Many hunters and target shooters believe strongly that, while the Second Amendment grants them the right to own and use firearms, inherent in that right is the responsibility to use them safely and carefully. According to the International Hunter Educa-

> " At the time the Constitution was written the United States was a very different place from what it is today. "

tion Association, there were 42 hunting fatalities in the United States and Canada combined in 2004.

This, say gun ownership proponents, is proof that responsible gun ownership is a reasonable expectation in modern society, even though people are no longer protecting their homesteads as they might have 200 years ago. Those who question whether the Second Amendment is as sweeping as gun owners say contend that even 42 fatalities are too many and that the only way to stop gun accidents is to curtail or completely eliminate private gun ownership.

> " Gun control supporters say that the availability of dangerous guns and ammunition—easy for a robber to steal, easy for a child to find—make any gun unsafe, no matter how careful and skilled the owner might be. "

Guns and Self-Defense

According to the U.S. Department of Justice's Bureau of Justice Statistics, 71 percent of all homicides were committed with some sort of firearm in 2005. It is not surprising that people would want to own guns for self-defense. The actual number of guns purchased for self-defense purposes is difficult to pin down. Some people are given guns that they ultimately use for self-defense. And sometimes otherwise honest people turn to illegal sources for weapons because they feel threatened and believe they cannot wait.

In his book *Big Bang: The Loud Debate over Gun Control*, Norman L. Lunger talks about the types of stories gun rights proponents like to share to illustrate the value of guns for self-defense:

> There's the woman in Washington State who grabbed a handgun and chased a burglar from her bedroom. And the convenience store clerk in Florida who shot a would-be robber in the chest. And the couple in Arkansas who were accosted by two would-be robbers outside their home and exchanged shots with them, killing one. . . . Gun rights supporters see this as proof of the effectiveness of guns in saving lives and property.[17]

Many gun rights supporters, in fact, say that the presence of a gun alone is usually enough to scare off criminals. Many criminals, even those who carry weapons, rely on fear and surprise to overcome their victims. If they know that their potential victims are themselves carrying guns, most criminals will avoid putting their own lives in danger.

Should So Many People Own Guns?

Gun control supporters say that the availability of dangerous guns and ammunition—easy for a robber to steal, easy for a child to find—make any gun unsafe, no matter how careful and skilled the owner might be. They claim that guns, whether kept for self-defense, for hunting, or for target shooting, create a real danger of theft or misuse. The Center for Gun Policy and Research at Johns Hopkins University reports that some 500,000 guns are stolen each year—meaning that each year a half million more illegal guns are being distributed to criminals. The *American Journal of Epidemiology* found in a 2004 study that keeping guns in the house, no matter how many or how carefully stored, raises the risk of homicide and suicide in the home.

Gun owners point out that the vast majority of people who own firearms are responsible and careful, and gun rights organizations such as NSSF and NRA provide safety training and gun education programs across the country. Just for hunters alone, each state has numerous regulations and requirements that determine where hunters may shoot, when they may hunt, and what they may hunt for. Responsible gun owners, they add, keep their firearms unloaded and locked. Gun control advocates acknowledge that many gun owners are safe and careful. At the same time, they point out, many gun owners are not as careful as they should be—and those who keep guns for self-defense may not choose to leave their weapons unloaded. The danger of accidental shootings (such as when a child finds a gun and fires at a playmate) or easy access to people who should not have guns (including those who have restraining orders against them, or those

> " Many gun rights supporters . . . say that the presence of a gun alone is usually enough to scare off criminals. "

who may be suicidal) is so great that tougher regulations against even "innocent" guns are necessary.

This is where the question of the Second Amendment's true intent comes into play. Does it guarantee the right of every American to own any kind of firearm—or does it give that right only to a limited number of people and only in limited circumstances? The American Civil Liberties Union is officially neutral on the issue of gun control precisely because of the Second Amendment's ambiguous wording; however, the organization takes the position that some regulation of gun purchases and ownership is acceptable. As the organization states:

> **[Gun control supporters] claim that guns . . . create a real danger of theft or misuse.**

We believe that the constitutional right to bear arms is primarily a collective one, intended mainly to protect the right of the states to maintain militias to assure their own freedom and security against the central government. In today's world, that idea is somewhat anachronistic and in any case would require weapons much more powerful than handguns or hunting rifles. The ACLU therefore believes that the Second Amendment does not confer an unlimited right upon individuals to own guns or other weapons nor does it prohibit reasonable regulation of gun ownership, such as licensing and registration.[18]

The needs of individuals have changed since the 18 century, and both sides of the issue are aware of this. Still, it remains difficult to determine whether it is truly constitutional for each U.S. citizen to own a gun, and each side of the issue has ample facts and figures to back up its claim. What is clear is that the debate is one that will go on for some time to come.

Primary Source Quotes*

Does the Constitution Guarantee the Right to Own Guns?

66 **There is no scenario when it's okay for government to come into my house and disarm me—not now, not ever.** 99

—Wayne LaPierre, speech to the National Rifle Association Annual Meeting, 2006. www.nra.org.

LaPierre is the executive vice president and CEO of the National Rifle Association.

....

66 **John Ashcroft will place the health and welfare of the NRA and its gun industry allies over that of the American public. What this means is simple: more assault weapons, less vigorous enforcement of federal gun laws, and a rollback of the Brady law.** 99

—Kristen Rand, statement opposing the choice of John Ashcroft for U.S. attorney general, January 4, 2001. www.vpc.org.

Rand is head of the Violence Policy Center.

....

* Editor's Note: While the definition of a primary source can be narrowly or broadly defined, for the purposes of Compact Research, a primary source consists of: 1) results of original research presented by an organization or researcher; 2) eyewitness accounts of events, personal experience, or work experience; 3) first-person editorials offering pundits' opinions; 4) government officials presenting political plans and/or policies; 5) representatives of organizations presenting testimony or policy.

66 Let me state unequivocally that the Second Amendment clearly protects the right of individuals to keep and bear firearms.... Like the First and Fourth Amendments, the Second Amendment protects the rights of 'the people.' 99

—John Ashcroft, letter to the NRA annual meeting, May 17, 2001. www.nraila.org.

Ashcroft is a former Republican U.S. senator from Missouri and also a former U.S. attorney general.

66 The Second Amendment makes it clear that an American citizen has an inherent right to bear arms unless he forfeits it through egregious criminal behavior. 99

—Edmund F. McGarrall, "More Laws, More Crime," *American Outlook,* Summer 2000.

McGarrall is a professor and director of the School of Criminal Justice at Michigan State University.

66 The Second Amendment makes no sharp distinction between the use of guns to resist oppression by the government and their use to resist oppression from which the government fails to protect us. 99

—Nelson Lund, "Taking the Second Amendment Seriously," *Weekly Standard,* July 24, 2000.

Lund is a professor at the George Mason University School of Law.

"We believe that the Constitution contains no barriers to reasonable regulations of gun ownership. If we can license and register cars, we can license and register guns."

—American Civil Liberties Union, "Why Doesn't the ACLU Support an Individual's Unlimited Right to Bear Arms?" March 4, 2004. www.aclu.org.

The American Civil Liberties Union works to ensure that the civil rights of all Americans are protected.

"The attitude of Americans toward the military was much different in the 1790's than it is today. Standing armies were mistrusted, as they had been used as tools of oppression by the monarchs of Europe for centuries."

—The U.S. Constitution Online, "Constitutional Topic: The Second Amendment." www.usconstitution.net.

The U.S. Constitution Online provides information about the U.S. Constitution and its role in American life.

"It would be absurd to say one has the right to life, but does not have the right to the means necessary to protect that life. It would be like saying one has the right to life, but not the right to purchase food. Yet, this is what opponents to the right to own a gun are really against: the right to life."

—Capitalism.Org, "FAQs About Gun Rights," November 23, 2006. www.capitalism.org.

Capitalism.org is a Web site dedicated to the concept of laissez-faire (minimal government interference in business) capitalism.

66 Law-abiding gun owners . . . fully understand the concept of licensing and registration; most agree with one-gun-a-month laws; and they rarely object to requirements for a background check. The tension arises because gun owners are not convinced that gun control supporters don't secretly harbor a ban agenda. 99

—Richard Aborn, *Focus on Gun Studies,* Second Amendment Research Center, Spring 2003. www.secondamendmentcenter.org.

Aborn is the former director of Handgun Control, Inc. (now the Brady Center).

66 Our best evidence on public opinion about firearms policy arises from the fact that 45 percent of American households own upwards of 250 million firearms, and that as many Americans engage in hunting and target shooting as in jogging and tennis. 99

—James B. Jacobs, *Focus on Gun Studies,* Second Amendment Research Center, Spring 2003. www.secondamendmentcenter.org.

Jacobs is the author of *Can Gun Control Work?*

Facts and Illustrations

Does the Constitution Guarantee the Right to Own Guns?

- All but six states—California, Iowa, Maryland, Minnesota, New Jersey, and New York—have language in their state constitutions that mentions the "right to bear arms."

- In addition to convicted felons and drug users, those restricted from owning or purchasing guns in the United States include illegal aliens, anyone who received a dishonorable discharge from the military, and anyone who renounces his or her U.S. citizenship.

- The 18.5 million hunters in the United States contribute more than $30 billion annually to the U.S. economy and support more than 986,000 jobs.

- Hunters are the primary financiers (more than $1.5 billion per year) of conservation programs that benefit all Americans who appreciate wildlife and wild places.

- Thirty-one states have "right-to-carry" gun laws. One such law allows certain people to carry concealed weapons.

- According to a 2001 report by the Johns Hopkins Center for Gun Policy and Research and the National Opinion Research Center, 54 percent of those surveyed favor both passing stricter gun control laws and the strict enforcement of the current and new laws. Fifty-five percent want laws against those who sell guns illegally to be tougher than for selling illegal drugs.

- No legislation regulating the private ownership of firearms has ever been struck down in the United States on Second Amendment grounds, according to the American Bar Association.

- The Second Amendment Foundation notes that only 1 out of every 6,500 handguns is used in a homicide.

Reasons for Rejecting Firearm Applications (FBI, 1999–2003)

More than half of gun applications between 1999 and 2003 were rejected because the applicant had a felony on his or her criminal record. Convicted felons are prohibited from owning firearms.

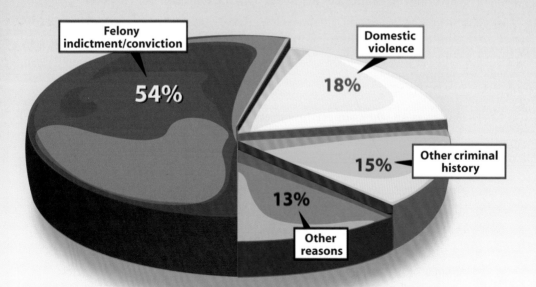

Source: U.S. Department of Justice, "Background Checks for Firearm Transfers," 2004. www.ojp.usdoj.gov.

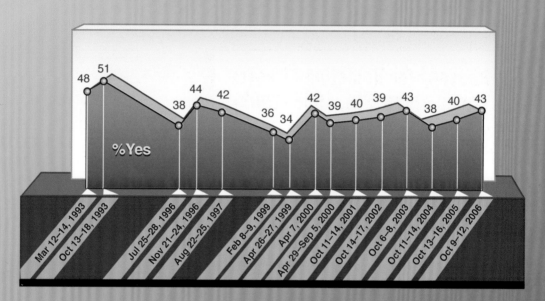

Americans Who Own Guns

Do you have a gun in your home?

%Yes

48, 51, 38, 44, 42, 36, 34, 42, 39, 40, 39, 43, 38, 40, 43

Mar 12–14, 1993 · Oct 13–18, 1993 · Jul 25–28, 1996 · Nov 21–24, 1996 · Aug 22–25, 1997 · Feb 8–9, 1999 · Apr 26–27, 1999 · Apr 7, 2000 · Apr 29–Sep 5, 2000 · Oct 11–14, 2001 · Oct 14–17, 2002 · Oct 6–8, 2003 · Oct 11–14, 2004 · Oct 13–16, 2005 · Oct 9–12, 2006

In October 2006, 43 percent of Americans had a gun in their home. This number is down from October 1993 when more than half of Americans had guns in their home. The number of gun owners has been increasing since October of 2004.

Source: The Gallup Poll, "Do You Have a Gun in Your Home?" 2006. www.galluppoll.com.

- A poll conducted by Zogby International in 2004 found that two-thirds of respondents believed there were enough gun control laws on the books and that these laws should be more vigorously enforced.

- According to figures reported by Sane Guns (a group that advocates for a sensible approach to gun control), 82 percent of Americans polled support police permits for all people who wish to purchase a gun, and 69.6 percent believe that handgun owners should be licensed and trained to use their weapons.

Reasons People Own Guns

Many people own guns for hunting and target practice. Gun control proponents point to the fact that each year there are deaths resulting from people using guns for target shooting and hunters who have accidentally shot another hunter, a bystander, or themselves. According to the International Hunter Education Association, there were 42 hunting fatalities in the United States and Canada combined in 2004. Gun rights supporters argue that it is unfair to punish people for mistakes.

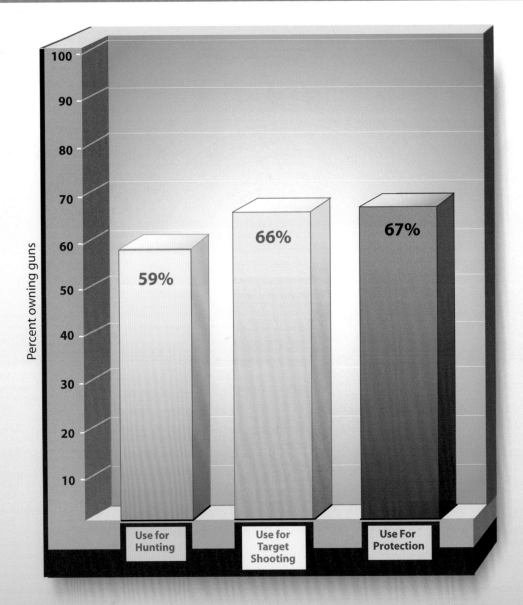

Percent owning guns

- Use for Hunting: 59%
- Use for Target Shooting: 66%
- Use For Protection: 67%

Source: The Gallup Poll, 2006. www.galluppoll.com.

Does the Constitution Guarantee the Right to Own Guns?

- According to the FBI, in the first 3 months of 2004, 13,116 people were denied gun purchases because they had prior convictions for crimes punishable by a minimum of 1 year in jail.

- According to the U.S. Department of Justices Crime Clock 2005, a violent crime occurred in the United in 2005 every 22.7 seconds.

Americans' Views of Gun Laws

In terms of gun laws in the United States, which of the following would you prefer to see happen?

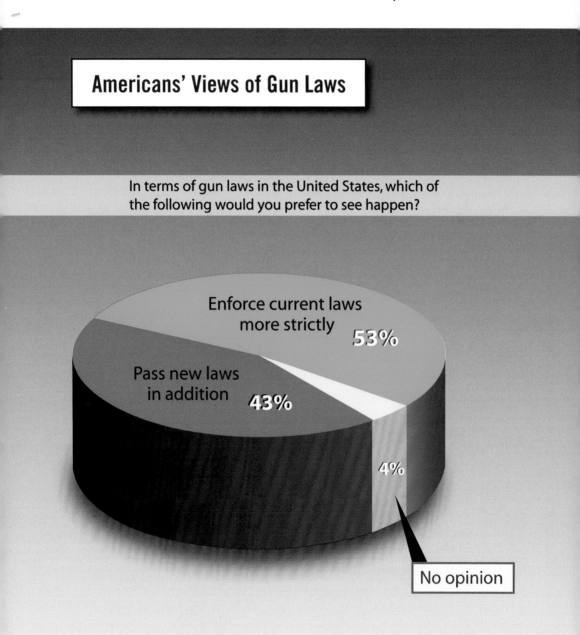

Enforce current laws more strictly **53%**

Pass new laws in addition **43%**

4%

No opinion

Source: The Gallup Poll, 2006. www.galluppoll.com.

Are Some Gun Bans Warranted?

❝When I watch TV and see small arms of the AK family in the hands of bandits, I keep asking myself: how did those people get hold of them?❞

—Mikhail Kalashnikov, inventor of the AK-47 and other firearms designed for military assaults, in a 2005 interview with Reuters.

Are there some guns that are so dangerous they should be banned from sale to the public? As of late 2006, there are no federal firearms bans on the books in the United States. Seven states—California, New Jersey, Hawaii, Connecticut, Maryland, Massachusetts, and New York—have their own weapons bans. In 1989 California became the first state to pass a weapons ban against certain assault weapons. New Jersey's ban, passed a year later, included a more comprehensive list of weapons than California's ban. The Massachusetts ban, passed in 1998, required anyone seeking to buy certain types of assault weapons to apply for a special license. New York's ban, passed in 2000, made it a felony to possess an assault weapon or large-capacity magazine.

These laws went above and beyond the Federal Assault Weapons Ban of 1994 (part of the Violent Crime Control and Law Enforcement Act), which banned the sale of several types of semiautomatic weapons. Its goal was to remove from the market any weapons that could be used by civilians in military-style attacks.

The Federal Assault Weapons Ban

The scope of the Federal Assault Weapons Ban was fairly wide. It specifically banned 19 weapons by name, including the Norinco, Mitchell, and

Poly Technologies Avtomat Kalashnikovs, the Beretta A470, the Colt AR-15, the Action Arms Israeli Military Industries UZI and Galil, and the Intratec TEC-9, TEC DC-9, and TEC-22. To ensure compliance, the ban also extended to copies or duplicates of these weapons. In addition, conventional firearms were prohibited from being manufactured with features commonly found on assault weapons. Rifles could not feature a bayonet mount, a protruding pistol grip, or a grenade launcher. Pistols could not have a magazine outside the grip, a threaded muzzle, or a barrel shroud. Shotguns could not include detachable magazines or a fixed magazine capacity of greater than five rounds.

Supporters of this law, including some gun rights enthusiasts, said that military-grade weapons, with their capacity to inflict enormous damage, represented too great a danger to public safety. The real danger of assault weapons, say their opponents, is that as long as they are available, they can always fall into the hands of criminals who can wreak havoc with them. The Brady Center to Prevent Gun Violence stated, "As more and more assault weapons are confiscated from crime scenes, fewer and fewer criminals and juveniles will have access to these deadly killing machines."[19]

> **Many of the features of [assault weapons] are of limited use at best to the average gun owner.**

Many of the features of these weapons are of limited use at best to the average gun owner. A barrel shroud, for example, cools the barrel so that a firearm can shoot rounds in rapid succession without danger of overheating. A threaded barrel or muzzle can hold a flash suppressor (which helps conceal the shooter after dark).

What Are Assault Weapons?

An assault weapon is a firearm that has been designed to inflict maximum lethal damage. Assault weapons are used in military combat situations, where soldiers are responsible for protecting themselves and their comrades. To understand what assault rifles can do, we can compare them with the typical hunting rifle just in the way each is fired. A hunting rifle is fired from the shoulder and requires the shooter to aim with pinpoint accuracy at a specific target. An assault rifle, on the other hand, can be hand-held which gives the shooter greater control and less need for exact accuracy.

Assault weapons include automatic and semiautomatic weapons. Automatic weapons (machine guns, for instance) will fire as long as the trigger is pressed or until the ammunition runs out. Semiautomatic weapons fire one round of ammunition and reload automatically with each pull of the trigger. Both automatic and semiautomatic weapons can be used for sustained attacks such as military assaults.

One argument that many gun control advocates make when calling for assault weapons bans is that the average shooter simply has no need for such massive firepower. They contend that one hardly needs an Uzi submachine gun to shoot a deer. Those who favor gun rights counter that this type of ban could easily be modified to include the hunting rifles of law-abiding citizens.

The 1994 Ban Expires

The 1994 assault weapons ban was written with a built-in sunset (expiration) clause. Although many members of Congress and President George W. Bush expressed their approval of the law, the president allowed it to sunset on September 13, 2004. Gun control advocates saw the law's expiration as a stunning loss, while gun rights advocates expressed satisfaction. Groups such as the NRA argue that the assault weapons ban was an unnecessary measure because it failed to address the real issue—criminals. In a fact sheet titled "Good Riddance to the Clinton Gun Ban," the NRA made the same claim it has made

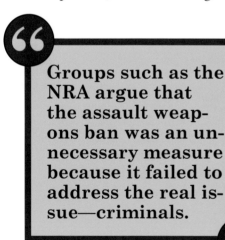

Groups such as the NRA argue that the assault weapons ban was an unnecessary measure because it failed to address the real issue—criminals.

for handguns and hunting rifles: "In a free society, the burden of proof is not upon those who wish to exercise rights, it is upon those who wish to restrict rights. Therefore, gun-ban supporters must show why the guns should be banned, and thus far they have not done so. It is clear that the guns are rarely used in crime, and rarely does the criminal's choice of gun determine the outcome of his crime."[20]

Banning Armor-Piercing Ammunition

Guns themselves are not deadly without ammunition, and some gun control advocates have taken up the cause of banning certain types of ammunition—in particular, "armor-piercing" bullets. Since 1986 it has been illegal for individuals in the United States to purchase, manufacture, or import armor-piercing bullets. Police and military uses and approved government testing are exempt from the ban. This specialized ammunition is designed to go through tanks, concrete barriers, and other protections too thick or strong for regular ammunition to penetrate. It can also go through protective body armor (such as bulletproof vests). Typically these bullets are made of special alloys that make them stronger and able to get through otherwise impenetrable material.

> While not gun control per se, ammunition bans, tracing tools, and technological gun innovations all serve the purpose of rendering guns unable to inflict bodily harm.

Gun rights advocates maintain that a ban on armor-piercing bullets can potentially infringe on the rights of innocent citizens. Most rifle ammunition can go through most body armor; gun owners fear that hunters could conceivably lose their right to buy ammunition. Others believe that the true danger of armor-piercing bullets to the general public has been exaggerated by the media. One law enforcement official who wrote an article in 2004 stated that the perceived danger is "a myth born from media hype and nurtured by unrealistic Hollywood portrayals and the deliberately misleading claims of the anti-gun lobby."[21]

Banning Other Ammunition

Some gun control advocates have tried to restrict the sale and manufacture of all ammunition, not merely armor-piercing bullets, as a means of curtailing gun violence. As of late 2006, several bills around the country were enacted that banned the sale of ammunition to certain individuals. In California, for example, legislation was under consideration that would require all purchases of ammunition to be conducted in person (rather than via mail order or over the Internet).

> **Some gun control advocates have embraced the idea of 'traceable' bullets, etched with a serial number that could lead to the purchaser.**

Some gun control advocates have embraced the idea of "traceable" bullets, etched with a serial number that could lead to the purchaser. There has been research into the creation of a "smart gun" that could read the owner's physical characteristics (such as an individual's grip) and prevent its operation by anyone else. While not gun control per se, ammunition bans, tracing tools, and technological gun innovations all serve the purpose of rendering guns unable to inflict bodily harm.

The question of whether gun bans are worthwhile, necessary, or even constitutional will continue to be debated by both sides of the gun control issue. It is important for both sides to look at the issue as rationally as possible—no easy task for such an emotional issue. But if past actions are any indicator, it seems reasonable to say that neither outright bans on all or most guns, nor outright elimination of all gun bans, serve citizens well.

Are Some Gun Bans Warranted?

❝ I am a hunter. I'm a gun owner. I'm also a former law enforcement officer. I ran one of the largest district attorney's offices in America. I know something about prosecuting. Most of the law enforcement agencies wanted that assault weapons ban. They don't want to go into a drug bust and be facing an AK-47. **❞**

—John Kerry, presidential debate with George W. Bush, Oct. 13, 2004.

Kerry (D-Mass) is a U.S. senator and was a presidential candidate in 2004.

....

❝ If the government takes our guns, it's not because they are trying to help us. It's because they are trying to control us. **❞**

—David Yeagley, "Warriors and Weapons," *FrontPage Magazine*. frontpagemag.com.

Yeagley is an adjunct professor of humanities at the University of Oklahoma and a Comanche Indian.

....

* Editor's Note: While the definition of a primary source can be narrowly or broadly defined, for the purposes of Compact Research, a primary source consists of: 1) results of original research presented by an organization or researcher; 2) eyewitness accounts of events, personal experience, or work experience; 3) first-person editorials offering pundits' opinions; 4) government officials presenting political plans and/or policies; 5) representatives of organizations presenting testimony or policy.

❝We talk about homeland security. We talk about possible terrorists in this country, and yet we make it so easy for those out there to buy guns.❞

—Carolyn McCarthy, speech before the U.S. House of Representatives, March 16, 2006.

McCarthy is a Democratic congresswoman from New York. She ran for Congress after her husband was killed and her son was seriously wounded in a 1993 gun attack on a suburban commuter train on Long Island.

❝Lee Harvey Oswald . . . used a mail-order Italian army surplus rifle. He had seen it advertised in the NRA's *American Rifleman* and ordered it for $19.95 ($21.45 with postage and handling.)❞

—Norman L. Lunger, *Big Bang: The Loud Debate over Gun Control.* Brookfield, CT: Twenty-First Century, 2002.

Lunger has written several books on history and public policy.

❝Few of us would sleep better at night knowing that anyone who passed a standard background check could acquire portable missiles capable of shooting down commercial jetliners or weapons of mass destruction such as nerve gas or atomic bombs.❞

—Philip L. Cook and Jens Ludwig, *Gun Violence: The Real Costs.* New York: Oxford University Press, 2000.

Cook is on the faculty of the Sanford Institute of Public Policy at Duke University. Ludwig is on the faculty of the Georgetown Institute of Public Policy.

❝Like tobacco, motorcycles, or prescription drugs, guns are undeniably dangerous products. Most Americans not only expect but demand that our government act to protect consumers from unsafe uses of perfectly legal products.❞

—John D. Cohen, "Smart Guns: Breaking the Gun Control Impasse," *PPI Backgrounder,* March 1, 2000.

Cohen is the director of the Progressive Policy Institute's Community Crime Fighting Project.

**❝At best, [smart gun technology is] an immature tech-
nology a great distance away from proving itself ap-
plicable to the guns used daily by police officers and
law-abiding armed citizens.❞**

—Massad Ayoob, "State of the Smart Guns," *Guns Magazine,* February 2001.

Ayoob is a veteran police officer and director of the Lethal Force Institute in New
Hampshire.

**❝We believe absolutely that guns should not be banned.
We believe that in our constitution, gun ownership is
protected just like freedom of speech, and the freedom
from cruel and unusual punishment.❞**

— Second Amendment Foundation, "FAQs: Gun Rights." www.saf.org.

The Second Amendment Foundation (SAF) is dedicated to promoting a better
understanding of what it notes is "our Constitutional heritage to privately own
and possess firearms."

**❝There never has been any such thing as a 'cop-killer'
bullet. The issue is a fiction, invented for purposes of
politics, not public safety.❞**

—David Kopel, *National Review Online,* March 1, 2004. www.nationalreview.com.

Kopel is director of the Independence Institute.

**❝Let's suppose that a total handgun ban . . . had a
chance of being enacted. . . . What about the 65 million
handguns Americans already own? Some law-abiding
gun owners would no doubt turn them in, but many or
most would not.❞**

—Cathy Young, "When Liberals Lie About Guns," *Salon,* March 13, 2000.

Young is an author and journalist. She is also a columnist for the *Boston Globe.*

Facts and Illustrations

Are Some Gun Bans Warranted?

- According to *Shooting Industry* magazine, in 2000, gun makers in the United States manufactured 3,763,345 firearms, including 1,281,861 handguns.

- According to the FBI, there are approximately 250 million firearms in private hands, with 5 million additional guns being purchased every year.

- There are close to 4 million assault weapons in the United States, which amounts to roughly 1.7 percent of the total gun stock.

- According to U.S. Department of Justice data (fiscal year 2000–2002), only 2 percent of federal gun crimes were actually prosecuted. Among the laws ignored are laws intended to punish illegal gun trafficking, firearm theft, and corrupt gun dealers.

- SKS assault rifles, which have been used in police killings, are the rifle model most frequently encountered by law enforcement officers, according to a 2002 report by the Federal Bureau of Alcohol, Tobacco, Firearms, and Explosives (ATF).

- Teflon coatings, which were touted as allowing bullets to penetrate further, were actually added to bullets to eliminate wear on the barrel of the firearm.

State Gun Control Laws

While most states have moderately lenient gun control laws, there are 5 states with very restrictive laws and 9 states with very lenient laws.

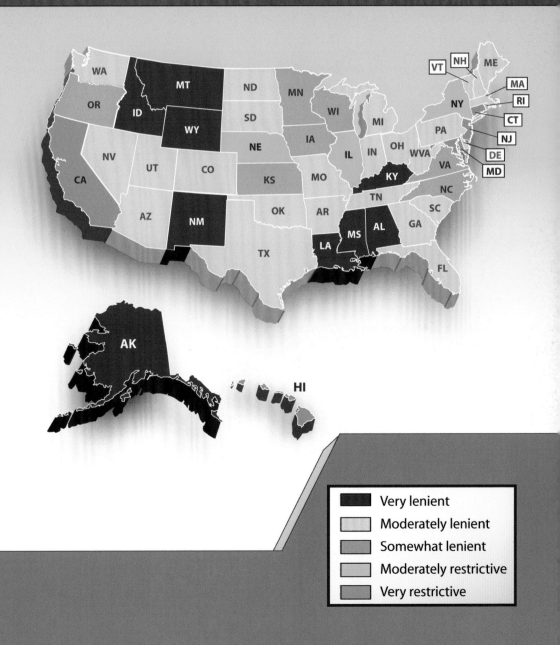

Very lenient
Moderately lenient
Somewhat lenient
Moderately restrictive
Very restrictive

Source: The Brady Campaign, "2004 Report Card." www.bradycampaign.org.

How Americans Feel About Assault Rifle Laws

Voters were asked their opinion on a law that would make it illegal to manufacture, sell, or possess semiautomatic guns. In all three years most Americans said they would support such a law, but support has declined from 59 percent in 2000 to 50 percent in 2004.

Are you for or against a law that would make it illegal to manufacture, sell, or possess semi-automatic guns known as assault rifles?

	For	Against	No Opinion
2004 October	50%	46%	4%
2000 October	59%	39%	2%
1996 August	57%	42%	2%

Source: The Gallup Poll, 2004. www.galluppoll.com.

- Kevlar vests worn by law enforcement officials are bullet-resistant, not bulletproof, according to the Bureau of Alcohol, Tobacco, Firearms, and Explosives. There are different levels of bullet resistance, but no armor is completely immune to bullets.

- According to the National Shooting Sports Foundation, accidental firearm fatalities are at an all-time low—down 60 percent over the last 20 years.

- Data compiled by the Bureau of Justice Statistics (U.S. Department of Justice) reveals that of 54 police officers killed by firearms in the line of duty in 2004, 36 were killed with handguns and 18 were killed with other types of guns.

- According to a poll conducted by Zogby International in 2004, 79 percent of those surveyed believed that individuals who have had firearms safety training and paid a licensing fee should be allowed to carry guns.

- A poll conducted by the National Association of Chiefs of Police found that 93 percent of respondents believed it was all right for individuals to possess firearms for sport or self-defense.

Assault Weapons: Gun Owners Versus Non–Gun Owners

The highest percentage of people who support stricter rules on assault weapons are non–gun owners, but more than half of gun owners also support stricter rules on assault weapons.

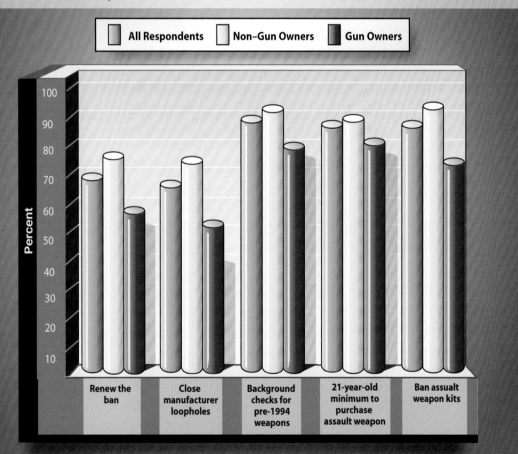

Source: Consumer Federation of America, "Consumers Strongly Support Renewing and Strengthening the Federal Assault Weapons Ban," 2004.

Key People and Advocacy Groups

James S. Brady: James S. Brady was press secretary to President Ronald Reagan. He was seriously wounded by John Hinckley during an attempt on Reagan's life on March 30, 1981. He and his wife Sarah (see below) have been active in the campaign to prevent gun violence by enacting stronger gun laws.

Sarah Brady: Sarah Brady became active in the gun control movement after her husband James (see above) was shot in March 1981. She was chair of Handgun Control, Inc. and later became chair of the Center to Prevent Handgun Violence. She has been an outspoken supporter of reducing gun violence through education and legal advocacy.

Paul Helmke: Paul Helmke, former mayor of Fort Wayne, Indiana, has been a strong supporter of gun control legislation throughout his public career. While mayor of Fort Wayne, he worked with local religious leaders to create "Stop the Madness," an antiviolence program geared toward youths. He has worked closely with James and Sarah Brady in their quest for stronger gun laws.

Charlton Heston: Academy Award–winning actor Charlton Heston has become known in his later years for his outspoken views on gun owners' rights. He was president of the National Rifle Association from 1998 to 2003, during which time he was an able and popular advocate for the role of guns and gun ownership in American society.

Suzanna Gratia Hupp: Suzanna Gratia Hupp is a member of the Texas state legislature and an outspoken proponent of individuals' right to carry concealed weapons. She watched her parents and 21 other patrons in a restaurant get shot 1991; although she owned a gun and had brought it with her, she had left it in the car to comply with state law.

Gary Kleck: Gary Kleck is a professor at the College of Criminology and Criminal Justice at Florida State University. He has written numerous books and journal articles based on research he and his colleagues have conducted, in which he claims that gun ownership or availability has little actual effect on violent crime and that guns used in self-defense may actually help reduce crime rates.

David B. Kopel: David B. Kopel, a policy analyst with the Cato Institute and research director of the Independence Institute, has written extensively on the topic of gun control, which he opposes. He believes that the Second Amendment affords all law-abiding citizens the right to own firearms.

Wayne LaPierre Jr.: Wayne LaPierre Jr. is executive vice president and CEO of the National Rifle Association. A member of the NRA since 1978, he has been the group's principal spokesman for more than two decades. LaPierre, who holds a degree in political science, is an avid sports shooter. He is also active in the North American Wetlands Conservation Council.

Carolyn McCarthy: Carolyn McCarthy is a Democratic U.S. representative who represents part of Long Island, New York. McCarthy's husband Dennis and son Kevin were shot by a disturbed passenger on a commuter train on December 7, 1993. Dennis died and Kevin was seriously wounded. McCarthy decided to run for Congress to push for stronger gun control laws.

Rebecca Peters: Rebecca Peters is director of the International Action Network on Small Arms (IANSA). She was active in the National Coalition for Gun Control, a group in her native Australia that helped strengthen that nation's antigun laws. Peters was previously involved with the Open Society Institute, a private organization that supports economic, legal, and social reform around the world.

Chronology

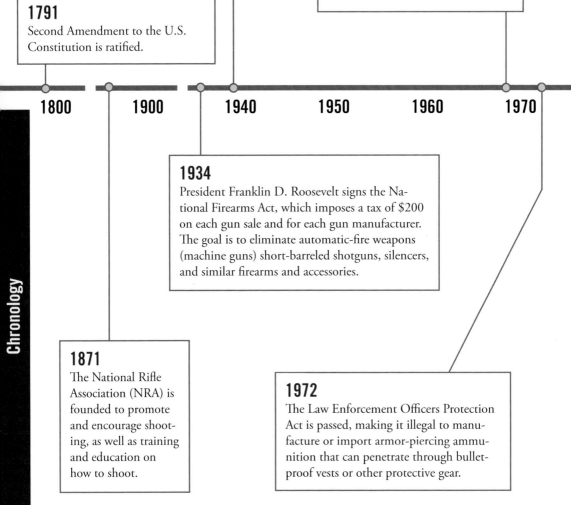

1938
The Federal Firearms Act is passed. This law requires anyone selling firearms through interstate or foreign channels to obtain a federal firearms license from the U.S. secretary of commerce, to record the names and addresses of all purchasers of guns, and to refuse to sell guns to those convicted of certain crimes or who lack a permit.

1968
Congress passes the Gun Control Act, which toughens the 1934 and 1938 laws. More gun dealers are required to keep records, and more detailed record keeping is also required. Handgun sales across state lines are restricted, and virtually all felons are banned from owning guns. Drug users, those deemed mentally incompetent, and some others are also prohibited from owning a gun.

1791
Second Amendment to the U.S. Constitution is ratified.

1800   1900   1940   1950   1960   1970

1934
President Franklin D. Roosevelt signs the National Firearms Act, which imposes a tax of $200 on each gun sale and for each gun manufacturer. The goal is to eliminate automatic-fire weapons (machine guns) short-barreled shotguns, silencers, and similar firearms and accessories.

1871
The National Rifle Association (NRA) is founded to promote and encourage shooting, as well as training and education on how to shoot.

1972
The Law Enforcement Officers Protection Act is passed, making it illegal to manufacture or import armor-piercing ammunition that can penetrate through bulletproof vests or other protective gear.

1993

The Brady Handgun Violence Prevention Act (the "Brady Bill") is passed. It imposes a five-day waiting period and background check for any unlicensed person who wishes to purchase a handgun. It requires a National Instant Criminal Background Check System to be administered by the FBI, which allows all checks to be done over the telephone or electronically.

2005

The Protection of Lawful Commerce in Arms Act is passed. It absolves gun dealers from culpability when a weapon is used to commit a crime.

1986

The Firearms Owners' Protection Act is passed. It eases restrictions on gun sales and gun sellers, but adds penalties to certain crimes committed with a gun and to those who illegally ship guns. It also bans the sale and manufacture of many machine guns.

2000

Legislatures in Oregon, Colorado, and New York pass laws that control the sale and handling of firearms, especially by youths.

U.S. gun makers mainufacture 3,763,345 firearms

1980   1985   1990   1995   2000   2005

1994

The Violent Crime Control and Law Enforcement Act (the "Assault Weapons Ban") is passed. It bans the manufacture, possession, and importation by civilians of new semiautomatic assault firearms and the ammunition used in such firearms. It also prohibits juveniles from possessing or selling handguns.

2004

President Bush allows the Violent Crime Control and Law Enforcement Act to sunset.

1981

March 30-James Brady, then press secretary to President Reagan, is severely wounded during an assassination attempt on the president. President Reagan is wounded in the head.

1996

Sears, JCPenney, Montgomery Ward, and Target stop selling firearms in part because of concern over keeping adequate records and in part because they fear liability for guns that are misused.

1999

Two high school students, Dylan Klebold and Eric Harris, drive to Columbine High School in Littleton, Colorado, on the morning of April 20, and open fire randomly on students and teachers. They kill 12 students and a teacher before killing themselves.

Related Organizations

American Civil Liberties Union (ACLU)

125 Broad St., 18th Floor

New York, NY 10004

phone: (212) 607-3300

fax: (212) 607-3318

Web site: www.aclu.org

The American Civil Liberties Union is a nonprofit nonpartisan organization that works to protect civil rights and liberties. It is officially neutral on the topic of gun control, but it believes that the Constitution has no barriers to reasonable gun regulation such as licensing and registration of firearms.

Armed Females of America

2702 E. University Dr., Suite 103

PMB213

Mesa, AZ 85213

phone: (480) 924-8202

Web site: www.armedfemalesofamerica.com

Armed Females of America is a gun rights organization that focuses on women who own guns. Its mission is to see all gun laws repealed, including the 1934 National Firearms Act (which taxes gun sales and gun manufacturers).

The Brady Campaign to Prevent Gun Violence / The Brady Center to Prevent Gun Violence

1225 Eye St. NW, Suite 1100

Washington, DC 20005

phone: (202) 898-0792 (Brady Campaign)

fax: (202) 371-9615 (Brady Campaign)

phone: (202) 289-7319 (Brady Center)

fax: (202) 408-1851 (Brady Center)

Web site: www.bradycenter.org

The Brady Campaign/Brady Center to Prevent Gun Violence is the nation's largest nonpartisan grassroots organization working to prevent gun violence. It encourages enforcement of existing laws and passage of legislation that will make it harder for guns to fall into the hands of criminals.

Centers for Disease Control and Prevention (CDC)

1600 Clifton Rd.

Atlanta, GA 30333

phone: (404) 639-3311 or (800) 311-3435

Web site: www.cdc.gov

The Centers for Disease Control and Prevention, an arm of the U.S. Department of Health and Human Services, compiles data on disease as well as injuries, including injuries from violent crime, crimes against youth, and suicide.

Doctors for Sensible Gun Laws

Web site: www.dsgl.org

Doctors for Sensible Gun Laws is a group of physicians who believe that, while some gun laws may be helpful, many are not, in part, they believe, because most gun violence is actually carried out in crime prevention, not the commission of crimes.

Gun Owners of America (GOA)

8001 Forbes Pl., Suite 102

Springfield, VA 22151

phone: (703) 321-8585

fax: (703) 321-8408

Web site: www.gunowners.org

Gun Owners of America is a nonprofit lobbying association dedicated to defending the Constitutional right of individuals to own guns as noted in the Second Amendment. It works to give its support for legislation and other government initiatives that protect gun owners' rights.

International Action Network on Small Arms (IANSA)

Development House

56-64 Leonard St.

London EC2A 4JX

United Kingdom

phone: 44-207-065-0870

fax: 44-207-065-0871

Web site: www.iansa.org

The International Action Network on Small Arms is a global network of groups dedicated to ending the proliferation and abuse of small firearms and light weapons, which are often used in violent confrontations against innocent civilians. It raises awareness about the issue of gun violence and works with local agencies to develop legislation and educational programs.

National Rifle Association (NRA)

11250 Waples Mill Rd.

Fairfax, VA 22030

phone: (800) 672-3888

Web site: www.nra.org

Founded in 1871, the National Rifle Association promotes gun safety through training and education. It strongly supports the belief that Americans have a constitutional right to own firearms and believes gun violence can be controlled by enforcing existing laws.

People for the American Way

2000 M St. NW, Suite 400

Washington, DC 20036

phone: (202) 467-4999 or (800) 326-7329

Web site: www.pfaw.org

People for the American Way is a nonprofit organization that seeks to support and protect democratic values and institutions. It conducts research and provides policy papers on a number of issues, including gun control and violent crime.

United States Department of Justice

950 Pennsylvania Ave., NW,

Washington, DC 20530

phone: (202) 514-2000

Web site: www.usdoj.gov

The U.S. Department of Justice is the federal agency charged with ensuring that laws are enforced and that all Americans receive equal justice under the law. Its agencies include the Bureau of, Alcohol, Tobacco, Firearms, and Explosives (ATF), which focuses on protection against violent criminal activity, and the Bureau of Justice Statistics (BJS), which compiles statistics on crime rates, violent crime, and gun use in criminal activities.

For Further Research

Books

Michael A. Bellesiles, *Arming America: The Origins of a National Gun Culture.* New York: Vintage, 2000.

Peter Harry Brown and Daniel G. Abel, *Outgunned: Up Against the NRA.* New York: Free Press, 2003.

Philip L. Cook and Jens Ludwig, *Gun Violence: The Real Costs.* New York: Oxford University Press, 2000.

Donna Dees-Thomases with Alison Hendrie, *Looking for a Few Good Moms: How One Mother Rallied a Million Others Against the Gun Lobby.* Emmaus, PA: Rodale, 2004.

David T. Hardy, *Origins and Development of the Second Amendment.* Southport, CT: Blacksmith, 1996.

John R. Lott Jr., *More Guns, Less Crime: Understanding Crime and Gun Control Law.* Chicago: University of Chicago Press, 2000.

Norman L. Lunger, *Big Bang: The Loud Debate over Gun Control.* Brookfield, CT: Twenty-First Century, 2002.

Richard Poe, *The Seven Myths of Gun Control.* Roseville, CA: Forum, 2001.

Josh Sugarman, *Every Handgun Is Aimed at You: The Case for Banning Handguns.* New York: New Press, 2001.

U.S. Department of Justice, *Project Safe Neighborhoods: America's Network Against Gun Violence.* Washington, DC: U.S. Department of Justice, 2004.

Periodicals

Donald Braman and Dan M. Kahan, "Overcoming the Fear of Guns, the Fear of Gun Control, and the Fear of Cultural Politics," *Emory Law Journal,* Fall 2006.

John Cochran, "Mayors Focus on the Right to Bear Arms," *CQ Weekly,* May 15, 2006.

Dave Davies, "Poll: City Not Alone in Wanting Gun Curbs," *Philadelphia Daily News,* September 6, 2006.

Richard Graham, "Gun Sales Hit a Wal: Wal-Mart Stops Selling Guns in Many Stores," *Sports Afield,* August 2006.

Guns Magazine, "Rights Watch: Ineffective Laws," July 2006.

Peter Hardin, "Bill to Revise Gun Show Laws Advances in House," *Richmond (VA) Times-Dispatch,* September 8, 2006.

Jet, "Mayors Band Together Against Guns," May 15, 2006.

Don B. Kates, "San Francisco's Latest Gun Grab," *Handguns,* August/September 2006.

John King, "The Gun Show Blues: At the Crossroad of Avarice and Desire," *Guns Magazine,* August 2006.

Julie Lewis, interview with Rebecca Peters, "Guns, Guts, and Nerves of Steel," *Law Society Journal,* April 2006.

Los Angeles Times, "Deadly, Intentional Ignorance on Guns," editorial, September 3, 2006.

Timothy D. Lytton, "The Sting," *Boston Globe,* August 27, 2006.

John Macfarlane, "We Used to Think of Guns as an American Problem," *Toronto Life,* February 2006.

James O.E. Norell, "The Global War on Guns," *American Rifleman,* April 2006.

Amit R. Paley, "Gun Seller's Case Reveals Hurdles of Enforcement," *Washington Post,* July 26, 2006.

Philadelphia Daily News, "Street to Teens: Don't Pull That Gun," July 28, 2006.

Michael J. Sniffen, "Gun Crime Threatens Positive Trend; Lawbreaking Is Lowest in Decades," *Chicago Sun-Times,* September 11, 2006.

Will Sullivan, "Packing Heat on the Hill," *U.S. News & World Report,* July 17, 2006.

Russ Thurman, "Victories, Yes, but We're Not Untouchable," *Shooting Industry,* July 2006.

Byron Williams, "The World Must Wonder How U.S. Can Tolerate Guns," *Oakland (CA) Tribune,* September 7, 2006.

Internet Sources

Brady Campaign to Prevent Gun Violence, "Assault Weapons Threaten Public Safety," 2006. www.bradycampaign.org/facts/issues/?page=aw_renew.

Susan M. Connor and Kathryl L. Weslowski, "'They're Too Smart for That!' Predicting What Children Would Do in the Presence of Guns," *Pediatrics,* February 2, 2003. http://pediatrics.aappublications.org/cgi/content/full/111/2/e109.

Chris Cox, "Pro-Gun Lip Service," National Rifle Association Institute for Legislative Action, August 24, 2006. www.nraila.org/Issues/Articles/Read.aspx?id=206&issue=047.

GunCite, "Is a Gun an Effective Means of Self-Defense?" October 18, 2003. www.guncite.com/gun_control_gcdgeff.html.

Diana Zuckerman, "News You Can Use on Kids and Violence," National Research Center for Women and Families, September 13, 2006. www.center4research.org/violenceh.html.

Source Notes

Overview: Understanding the Debate

1. Deborah Homsher et al., "Gun Laws and Policies: A Dialogue," *Focus on Law Studies,* vol. 18, no. 2, Spring 2003. www.abanet.org.
2. George W. Bush, presidential debate with Senator John Kerry in Tempe, Arizona, OnTheIssues, October 13, 2004. www.issues2000.org.
3. John R. Lott Jr., *More Guns, Less Crime: Understanding Crime and Gun Control Laws.* Chicago: University of Chicago Press, 2000, pp. 10–11.
4. Children's Defense Fund, "Gun Report Reveals 2,827 Child and Teen Deaths by Firearms in 2003 Exceed U.S. Combat Deaths During Three Years in Iraq," June 13, 2006. www.childrens defense.org.
5. National Shooting Sports Foundation, Project ChildSafe, "FAQs," November 23, 2006. www.projectchildsafe.com.
6. National Rifle Association, Institute for Legislative Action, "Eighteen Million Kids Safer," July 27, 2006. www. nraila.org.
7. Violence Policy Center, "Joe Camel with Feathers: How the NRA with Gun and Tobacco Industry Dollars Uses Its Eddie Eagle Program to Market Guns to Kids," November 1997. www.vpc.org.

Can Gun Control Reduce Crime?

8. James Brady, "Brady Campaign Launches Comprehensive Effort Against Illegal Drugs," Brady Campaign to Prevent Gun Violence, March 30, 2006. www. bradycampaign.org.
9. Henry Waxman, letter to Paul O'Neill, April 18, 2002. www.democrats.reform. house.gov.
10. Charley Reese, "Owning a Gun," Gun Owners of America, October 2006. www.gunowners.org.
11. Legal Community Against Violence, "Gun Laws Do Make a Difference: An Analysis of the October 2003 CDC Study Evaluating the Effectiveness of Firearms Laws," October 2003. www. lcav.org.

Could Gun Control Reduce Youth Violence?

12. American Academy of Pediatrics, press release, 2004. www.aap.org.
13. Associated Press, "1.7 Million Kids Live in Homes with Loaded Guns," September 16, 2005.
14. National Rifle Association, Institute for Legislative Action, "2006 Fact Sheet." www.nraila.org.

Does the Constitution Guarantee the Right to Own Guns?

15. Second Amendment Foundation, "A Quick Primer on the Second Amendment," November 3, 2006. www.saf. org.
16. Brady Campaign to Prevent Gun Violence, "The Second Amendment," November 3, 2006. www.bradycam paign.org.
17. Norman L. Lunger, *Big Bang: The Loud Debate over Gun Control,* Brookfield, CT: Twenty-First Century, 2002, pp. 129–30.

18. American Civil Liberties Union, "Why Doesn't the ACLU Support an Individual's Unlimited Right to Keep and Bear Arms?" March 4, 2002. www.aclu.org.

Are Some Gun Bans Warranted?

19. Brady Campaign to Prevent Gun Violence, "The Assault Weapons Ban: Frequently Asked Questions." www.bradycampaign.org.

20. National Rifle Association, Institute for Legislative Action, "Good Riddance to the Clinton Gun Ban," May 22, 2004. www.nraila.org.

21. Mike Casey [pseud.], "Cop-Killer Bullets," GunCite, October 31, 2004. www.guncite.com.

List of Illustrations

Index

Aborn, Richard, 60
Ambulatory Pediatric Association, 36–37
American Academy for Child and Adolescent Psychiatry, 45
American Academy of Pediatrics, 37, 43, 46
American Association for the Surgery of Trauma, 37
American Civil Liberties Union (ACLU), 56, 59
American College of Emergency Physicians, 37
American Journal of Epidemiology, 55
American Public Health Association, 37
Americans for Gun Safety Foundation (AGSF), 31
    on federal gun trafficking prosecutions, 32
ammunition, restrictions on, 69–70
armor-piercing bullets, 11, 69
Ashcroft, John, 57, 58
assault rifles/weapons
    definition of, 67–68
    laws prohibiting, opinions on, 76 (chart)
        of gun owners vs. non-owners, 77(chart)
    regulation of, 66–67
    SKS, 74
    in U.S., numbers of, 74
Australian Bureau of Statistics, 31
automatic weapons, 15
Ayoob, Massad, 73

background checks
    FBI program for, 13
        limitations of, 22

gun sales taking place without, 32
    numbers performed and gun sales denied from, 22, 31
Big Bang (Lunger), 54
Bill of Rights, 51
Brady, James, 13, 23, 24
Brady, Sarah, 13
Brady Center to Prevent Gun Violence, 37
    on assault weapons, 67
Brady Handgun Violence Act (1993), 12–13, 21
    effects of
        on nonfatal gun-related crime, 32 (chart)
        on violent crime, 33 (chart)
bullet-resistant vests, 76
bullets
    armor-piercing, 11, 69
    Teflon coating of, 74
Bureau of Justice Statistics, U.S., 31, 54
Bush, George W., 16, 30
Bush, Laura, 44

Capitalism.org, 59
Center for Gun Policy and Research, 23, 61
Centers for Disease Control and Prevention (CDC), 25
    on murders of youth, 46
Child Access Prevention (CAP) laws, 38
children
    arrests of, for weapons possession, 48 (chart)
    arrests rates for weapons violations by, 47 (chart)
    effects of school shooting reports on, 44

About the Author

George A. Milite writes about a variety of issues in the social sciences. He is on the adjunct faculty at The New School in New York and an instructor at Temple University in Philadelphia. The author wishes to thank Deborah R. Stein for her invaluable research and editorial assistance.